SELF-DECLARATIONS
Volume 2
60 Day Devotional

Derrell L. Dean

Scriptures are from the *Holy Bible*, New King James Version© 1982 by Thomas Nelson Inc. Used by permission. All rights reserved. Scripture quotations marked (KJV) are taken from the King James Version.

Published in the United States by CreateSpace Inc.

Library of Congress Cataloging-in-Publication Data

Dean, Derrell L.

Self-Declarations Volume 2: 60 Day Devotional/Derrell L. Dean

Pages cm

ISBN: 1973711400 (electronic)
ISBN-13: 978-1973711407 (hardcover)

DEDICATION

This devotional book is dedicated to my parents Mr. and Mrs. Jerry and Linda Dean—your presence, prayers and belief in me has blessed my life tremendously. I pray that God allows me to continually make you proud and thank you for the sacrifices you made to raise my brothers and me.
To my brothers, Jerrell and Lenell –Thank you for never a dull moment. I pray that you will forever pursue the gifts and talents that God has given you.
To the Dirton, Dean, Strange and Reid Families—I love you all. I honor all of you for your love, support and commitment to each other and the spirit of togetherness.
To my church families—Fairfield United Methodist Church and Long Branch Baptist Church- Thank you for your encouragement and prayers. I'm thankful that God connected us in worship. Let's go higher!!

In Loving Memory of my grandparents—Mrs. Mary Dirton, Mr. Henry Dirton, and Mr. James Odell and Mrs. Mamie Reid-Dean

Blessings

CONTENTS

PREFACE

Well, God has done it again. He has spoken to His Servant to "Declare" unto us the power of WORDS that come forth from our mouths. When the Lord declares a thing, it comes to pass. Minister Derrell Dean explains to us in a clear way the power that God has granted unto us.

Genesis 2:19 says "…and brought them to Adam to see what he would CALL them. And whatever Adam CALLED each living creature, that was its NAME." Wow, God created the creatures, but gave Adam the responsibility, honor, and privilege to name each creature. God is still allowing us to declare and name the things that are brought before us. It may look like a problem, but you can declare or name it an opportunity. It may seem like lack, but you can declare or name it more than enough. It may look like a burden, but you can declare or name it the key to your blessing.

I encourage you to use this guide as a roadmap to better language, attitude, and future. Speak your way into your next blessing. God is waiting with anticipation to hear what you will name that which comes your way. I declare your future to be blessed and your faith to be unwavering. Speak Life! Speak Faith! Speak Hope! Speak the Word!

Pastor Sean Dogan

Long Branch Baptist Church

SELF-DECLARATIONS: VOLUME 2

60 DAY DEVOTIONAL

Day 1

"I AM PROTECTED"

"But the Lord is faithful, who will establish you and guard you from the evil one."

-2 Thessalonians 3:3

Thank God for His protection. My friends, every day that you and I live, we are experiencing the protection of God. There's no doubt in my mind that every moment we live and move, that He's keeping us. God's protective hand is in our lives when you and I arose this day, left the premises of our homes, travel to various destinations throughout the course of the day and return safely.

The truth of the matter is that all of us can witness to ways that God has shielded us from things externally and internally that could have brought detriment to our well-being. As a child, I remember my grandfather using an old two-story building as a barn to milk cows and store hay for the winter season. Being the rambunctious child at that time, I was always getting into something, to my own trouble. One time, I had the bright idea to climb up to the second story and jump onto the ground level or on the nearby trailer used to transport hay. I distinctly remember jumping down to the ground and landing on my feet to my amazement! Well of course, accomplishing that great feat once was not good enough. I had to do it again. The second time around, I had more confidence because I knew that if I did it before, I could surely do it again. I made the second jump and I remember landing on my feet but still stumbling to the ground. Much to my shock, nothing was broken or twisted but it was not as smooth even though I was protected.

In another instance, the four-year-old me wanted to ride my tricycle on an open porch and rolled off one side and broke my right arm. The pain was unbelievable, but it was necessary. Necessary? Yes, it was necessary for me to learn the lesson of being more careful in my actions. Out of both situations, I was protected.

We experience His protection all around us. I believe that we experience it driving on dangerous highways, surviving accidents with minor scrapes and even flying across the airways on those silver birds. For someone it may have been escaping an abusive relationship with the one you thought would never do you harm, but it happened. In all those cases, trivial things could have happened that should have ended with different results, but thanks be to God they did not.

The Apostle Paul writes to the Thessalonians in 2 Thessalonians 3:5 about God's protection stating, "But the Lord is faithful, who will establish you and guard you from the evil one." He gives the assurance that our God is faithful to protect those whom He watches over. For God to establish you means that He settles those of us who believe in Him from the chaos that this world creates. An established mind finds peace and safety in a faithful God. A mature mind might readily say that there used to be a time that you knew you were not as settled in your decision making. Now you have the testimony that the Lord himself has brought you too far for you to negate the fact that He's matured, established and settled you.

Not only will He establish you, but He'll guard you from the evil one! Now as your day starts, there will be spirits that you will encounter in a negative light. They will try with all their might to huff and puff and blow your house down. They will seek to bring damage to your character. They will be desirous of viewing your downfall. They will do their best to get to your mental capacity, but my earnest prayer is that they will not succeed. Why? Because God's protective and permissive power will not let it be so.

Today's Declaration Challenge: As you read about God's protection, I pray that you let your mind receive the protection that only God can give. I challenge you to look over your journey and all that you've overcome and survived. The fact that you survived things that others did not make it through, is a testament to God's guarding power. I challenge you to receive the divine protection of a good Heavenly Father that desires for you to do miraculous things. Don't let the mistakes of yesterday cause you to stop moving. If God gave you protection from the snares of the enemy, He'll also protect you from yourself. He'll keep you from keeping yourself down. Today declare **"I am protected."**

Notes

I am protected, I made it through some troubling things, and God made sure I wouldn't die.

Day 2

"I AM DRIVEN"

"I press toward the goal for the prize of the upward call of God in Christ Jesus."

-Philippians 3:14

To be or not to be? That is the question. One distinguishing quality of anyone or group that has accomplished remarkable things has always been that they were driven in all things pertaining to their dreams. They were unstoppable in their pursuit and sure of their goals.

To have a drive or be passionate about something is the key to achieving goals and succeeding at anything in life. The truth of the matter is that even the most driven individuals encountered failure at some points in their pilgrimage. Trust me when I tell you that every prize-winning cake baker has had some flops that didn't rise to the occasion. Every CEO has had days when they didn't make chiefly decisions. Every great singer has hit some sour notes in their day and most star athletes have watched their golden medal be given to someone else due to not completing their trial at the top of the line.

The idea of reaching for the prize or a goal is something that we as believers and even should all be familiar with. Our daily desire as born-again believers should be to live a life where we reach heaven's gates when this life is over. Even while we live, we are called to pursue milestones, godly lives and dreams that only God can bring us to. This driven characteristic or goal filled life is notated in the scriptures as Philippians 4:14 NKJV reads, "I press toward the goal for the prize of the upward call of God in Christ Jesus." Paul writes to inform the believers that we should not be "backward" in our thinking but rather be "forward." He gives his audience the inclination that they should be visionaries and that their eyes should be fixed on a higher, upward call.

It's nothing worse than being around someone who is backwards all the time. They are small minded in their thoughts. They can never see what's ahead because their heads are turned backwards. Might I suggest to you that it's dangerous to be entrenched around backwards thinking people. Progression is uncomfortable for such persons. They fear change and growth. Honestly speaking, for you and me to be driven we must make moves when we don't want to. When you have a *drive* in you, you don't march to the beat of someone else's drum. When you have a drive in you, you can't always put it into words the things that you do, but you know it feels right when you do it. Ask that graduate with multiple degrees how they attained them all and they'll tell you that they felt an internal push that wouldn't let them slow up even if their feet got tired. For that survivor of substance abuse that made a complete 180-degree turnaround to a better life, they'll tell you that even during their troubles, something drove them down a new road to recovery and they did not turn back.

My sisters and brothers, what drives you today? What motivates you to get things done? Is it a desire to finish strong or a desire to make others proud? Are you driven by a will to give God the glory in all things? Do you desire to make God look good? Let's be honest some people are driven with negative intentions and God is not motivated by our greed or selfishness but rather our selflessness. Those who purpose in their heart to be driven only for personal fame or notoriety, only achieve certain levels of success and never fully prosper. Stay driven to do that thing **today** that **yesterday** talked you out of finishing.

Today's Declaration Challenge: I challenge you to never lose your drive. Be encouraged that what you stand to gain is greater than anything you may have lost. Be challenged to keep your goals in sight and God by your side. Don't stop your car (your life) in a place that God meant for you to keep passing through. One that is driven knows where they are going and will not stop until they get there. Drive on my friends drive on and daily declare **"I am driven."**

Notes

Driven to enroll back in school
Obtain my dental hygiene degree
obtain my C.L.E.
Driven to make God proud!

Day 3

"I AM A NEW CREATURE"

"Therefore, if anyone is in Christ, he is a new creation; old things have passed away; behold all things have become new."
-2 Corinthians 5:17

From the time of our birth, you and I were born as new creatures without any presuppositions, formulated ideas or notions. We were brand new. Newly conceived into a world where things were already underway. Newly born with a fresh slate to become someone unique and special. A baby does not get the chance to decide how they are born, or what family they're born into. You just grow up and try to make the most out of what you're given. With that said, things happen in your early life that shape who you eventually grow up to become and what you choose to do.

You and I have choices into the course of our life whether they be good or bad. From those early decisions, as new creatures we are prone to make mistakes. It is inevitable. When mistakes and issues arise, we as human beings need a fresh start. We need that clean slate again, such as when we were born. As life would have it, we would be exposed to a new life in Christ whether it be from a church, friend, family member or an evangelical televised program that led you in a prayer of salvation. Oh, the joy that flooded your soul from such a decision. If we would be so compelled to come to

Christ, and accept Him as our Savior, we then become anew as believers in a God that can do the impossible.

This idea of being made a new creature even perplexed Nicodemus, a ruler of the Pharisees, who came to Jesus by night and asked him "How can a man be born when he is old? Can he enter a second time into his mother's womb and be born?" Jesus answered "Most assuredly, I say to you unless one is born of water and the Spirit, he cannot enter the kingdom of God. That which is born of the flesh is flesh, and that which is born of the Spirit is spirit. Do not marvel that I said to you, 'You must be born again." (John 3: 4-7). Jesus ultimately calls us all to a new life in Him if we would allow him. The choice is ours. We must want a difference to see a difference.

Paul the Apostle writes about this very thing in 2 Corinthians 5:17 saying "If anyone is in Christ, he is a new creation; old things have passed away behold all things have become new." Having Christ within replaces any trace of the enemy in our lives. It's a replacement of roles. When Christ is welcomed in, the works of the devil are excluded out. The old me then gives way to the new me. Throughout this day, I pray that you are operating in the "new creature" that God has called you to be and not the "old creature." When reminders of your past want to be present in your future let them know that you are a new creature.

Today's Declaration Challenge: Be encouraged to walk in the newness of God. I challenge you to daily take steps to put away your old way of doing things, to guard your way of speaking and even your old thoughts towards new situations. As a new creature in Christ, things will try their best to bring you down but keep your head up and your eyes focused in all things. You are not your past. You don't wear those clothes anymore. Walk in the newness of God and declare **"I am a new creature."**

Notes

_____

_____

_____

_____

_____

_____

_____

Day 4

"I AM COVERED"

"He shall cover you with His feathers and under His wings you shall take refuge, His truth will be your shield and buckler."

-Psalm 91:4

I believe in the covering power of God. I, like many others, can testify that He's covered me from situations that could have and should have ended my story. On my way to a worship service, I saw this firsthand. It was a very rainy Sunday morning in Upstate, SC and while journeying on the highway, my car went hydroplaning from a patch of rain water, from the strong depressing rain.

I lost control and the vehicle immediately veered right and off the road into a guardrail. As I braced for the impact, I remember screaming "Jesus" with a loud voice. Well, one odd fact happened. When I opened my eyes, the car had stopped, and I felt absolutely nothing after the impact. I never felt the impact between the guardrail and my vehicle though they did connect. In that very moment, God covered me. He had angels with me because it could have and should have been worse.

As you read that moment from my personal experience, I'm sure you can witness to times that God covered you as well. Whether it was in a freak accident that completely caught you by surprise or something that caused grief after a prolonged period, it did not prevail over you. The writer of Psalm 91 no doubt knows about the power of being covered. They write from the premise of God being strong, mighty and a refuge in our distress. The author declares in Psalm 91:3 "Surely He shall deliver you from the snare of the fowler." A fowler is used here symbolically as one who catches birds. The idea is that the enemy's job is to catch us and set traps for us to fail. There's much comfort in knowing that even though we know about the ways of evildoers, we have a deliverer in God.

The covering of God is what we all need today and every day. Just like the child caught out in the pouring rain that runs to find safety, every child of God needs a covering. For those of us who serve God and others in ministry roles, we should always desire to be covered by another leader who watches over your soul and prays to God on your behalf. It's the job of a pastor, undershepherd, ministry leader and church to watch over and cover those who serve among you. We do recognize God as the ultimate shepherd over our lives as Psalm 91:4 reads "He shall cover you with His feathers, and under His wings you shall take refuge."

As you live today and trek from here to there, let God's wings cover you. When you arise in the morning and you lie down at night, thank God for covering you. My prayer for you is that you find safety in God. Every child of God needs a covering. It matters not how mature you think you are or even if you just left one place of covering. Soon find another place of safety that only God can give. Rest and know that He won't let the traps of your enemy work. "No weapon formed against you shall prosper" (Isaiah 54:17).

Today's Declaration Challenge: I challenge you to find joy in God's covering grace. Be encouraged that even when life becomes troublesome, that God will send His strength to guard your life. Let God cover you. When He covers you, you have no reason to fear what comes at you. When He covers you, you have no reason to give up. I dare you to thank God for covering you from your own decisions and mistakes. Since God has covered you, you have the right to live for Him and prosper under His umbrella. Declare today **"I am covered."**

Notes

_____

_____

_____

_____

_____

_____

_____

Day 5

"I AM CONTRITE"

"The sacrifices of God are a broken spirit, a broken and a contrite heart. -These, O God, you will not despise."

-Psalm 51:17

Only the contrite can be fully used by God. Having a contrite heart and spirit can be one of the best things for a child of God to have. One might say that such a statement is ludicrous, but I beg to differ.

Being contrite means to be broken, remorseful or sorrowful. It's an attribute of someone who recognizes the error of their ways. When parents properly discipline their children, a contrite spirit comes over them as they shed tears of sorrow after being corrected for something that they've done. When a relationship that seemed to last the test of time dissolves, at least one of the person's involved will endure a state of contrition.

In my younger days as a kid, I easily recall the trouble I would find myself in for talking back or doing something mischievous that resulted in my own contrite spirit. It was in that moment that I had a choice to make. I could choose to either learn my lesson and not repeat the same act or suffer more graver consequences. That choice was all mine. If it had not been for the breaking moments, I would not have matured to make wiser decisions later.

The state of contrition or brokenness should have happened to all of us as believers at the time of our salvation or restoration with God. To know that God the Father sent His Only Son to save us from a world of sin and shame is a humbling thing. That's why if you're like me, the presence of God's Spirit in worship will bring me to a state of brokenness. Hands will go up, tears may flow and even cries may be heard as a sign that we need the help of our Savior. When God's presence shows up like that, it reminds me of my imperfections in the presence of a perfect God.

The psalmist David writes about this all too well in Psalms 51:17 as he has gone through a personal crisis with his own sin of taking a man's wife and then proceeded to take that same man's life. He pleads with God to not take His Spirit from him and admits his sinful ways, while acknowledging what God accepts from us as His people. He says "The sacrifices of God are a broken spirit. A broken and a contrite heart-These, O God, You will not despise." It's amazing to know that in our broken state God will not turn us away. I believe that my opening line is true for this day in that God can fully use the contrite and broken.

When was the last time you were contrite? When was the last time you felt a sense of brokenness? There's nothing to be ashamed of if you have. It's quite natural honestly. You may be in that place today. If you're currently in a place of contrition, it may be just where you need to be. The state you're in is not punishment but rather a time of refocusing your perspective and purpose. Let your tears flow. Let your heart cry out and then gather yourself today knowing you serve a God that's using this present moment for your development.

Today's Declaration Challenge: I encourage you to use the moments of contrition to come back to God, to trust Him again. I challenge you to believe Him to turn your mess into a message. Be encouraged to know your past was a setup for a great future. If a broken crayon can still color, a broken life can still prosper. Your brokenness is a platform for your rediscovery of your life. Today speak over yourself and say, **"I am contrite."**

Notes

I was contrite today - 5-15-18.
I cried and praised & worship
in the car before work. Asking
God forgiveness.

Day 6

"I AM FOUNDATIONAL"

"For no other foundation can anyone lay than that which is laid, which is Jesus Christ."

-1 Corinthians 3:11

Every person needs a good foundation in their life. To be successful, you need a basis of support to undergird you through the channels of life. For that very reason, a good parent engulfs themselves in the lives of their children. They do that to let them know that no matter how far you go in life to never forget where you come from and if you need any reminders they'll be right there.

I'll never forget many years ago when my parents dropped my twin brother and I off at college. Once we moved into our dorm room and before they left, my mother gave us the rundown of things to remember like going to bed on time, setting your alarm clock, paying attention in class and making good decisions. It was a speech every parent or guardian or relative gives to their child as they're coming of age and beginning to live separately from their "foundation." Though I can't recall everything word for word that was relayed to me, the big picture I made sure I caught. She was saying never forget the standards, morals and words of instruction and correction that they gave to us while we were with them. I believe also ultimately, we were given a mandate to continually seek God as our foundation.

My parents were in retrospect being foundational for my brothers and me. They were ensuring that we did not forget about the God of our salvation and the Lord of our lives. Paul drops this bit of knowledge to the Corinthians in 1 Corinthians 3:11 when it reads "For no other foundation can anyone lay than that which is laid, which is Jesus Christ." He lets them know that no matter where you go, what you do or even try to build, you need Christ as the center of your foundation.

Does that mean that today you won't face heartache with Christ as your foundation? No. Will you be bypassed from all drama? No. It does mean that God through Jesus will settle you even in tumultuous situations. With Him as your foundation, you and I won't lose our heads. Isaiah 28:16 reads "Therefore thus says the Lord God: "Behold I lay in Zion a stone for a foundation, a tried stone, a precious cornerstone, a sure foundation; Whoever believes will not act hastily."

One who is foundational is mindful of how they started, what it took to progress and what it takes to remain in the game. They are also aware of their present circumstance and the tenacity it takes to stay rooted.

Today's Declaration Challenge: Are you founded upon the ways of God today? Regardless of how you were brought up, if you give your heart back to God He settles you like no other. Be challenged to stand your ground today. Affirm what you were taught over yourself. Even if you must uproot some things and start over, make sure your next place is solid upon your faith in God. Declare today, no matter what comes against you **"I am foundational."**

Notes

Start pack school and be foundational.

Day 7

"I AM STILL-STANDING"

"Stand fast therefore in the liberty by which Christ has made us free
and do not be entangled again with a yoke bondage."

-Galatians 5:1

Your testimony may be complex. Your story may be long, but one thing should be consistent and that is that you're surviving it. Today may be a day of extraordinary joy for you. You may have just started the thing you've desired to do for years or began that career that you've been praying about. You may be in the middle of a season of flourishing and days of overflow.

On the opposite side of the coin you may be experiencing the worst pain in your life. Life may have troubled your heart in such a way that you don't know how you're going to make it. There may be more against you than for you. I dare you to look at either parallel and witness that whether you're in a great season or a troublesome one to find joy in the very fact that you're still standing.

The fact that you're still standing is an indication of many things. It firstly tells you that there is still much purpose in you. Secondly, it shows you're stronger than you think and lastly it lets you marvel that what you're up against did not take you out. The Apostle Paul writes from a vantage point of this very thing.

By telling the Galatians in Galatians 5:1 to "Stand fast

therefore in the liberty by which Christ has made us free and do not be entangled again with a yoke of bondage" he seeks to keep them focused in faith. My brothers and sisters, you and I can quickly witness that we are not who we used to be. Whether it was by choice or by force we had to change. In fact, you know that you're not the same when you don't even think the same way that you used to. Change is necessary for us all. To press on past our own issues and struggles we had to change and keep living.

Having Christ as our Savior, enables us to keep standing. He keeps us going. Praying to Him helps us survive and endure. With Christ as your anchor, you cannot fail. Any failure that we find ourselves in would then be our choice. If Christ made us free, he did so with a hope that we would find a new life in Him and pursue greater works. No one who is free looks for ways to be bound again unless they're not totally free in their mind.

You may have started today in a routine way of doing things but keep standing. You may suffer hardships to your destiny but keep standing. Symbols of your past may try to bring your past into your future but keep standing. You are not the same so keep standing. Keep believing for greater in your existence. As you stand, others may be sitting and complaining but again my friend, keep standing. Your choice to stand in Christ has everything to do with your survival and nothing to do with your doubters.

Today's Declaration Challenge: I challenge you to keep standing for what you believe in. I pray that you are not entangled again by any form of bondage. I speak over your life today that yesterday's bondage cannot match today's freedom over your life. You may have to stand around your enemies but keep it up. Nothing confuses opposition more than their inability to determine your next move. Today declare **"I am still-standing."**

Notes

_____

_____

_____

_____

_____

_____

_____

Day 8

"I AM EXPECTANT"

"The Lord is good to those who wait for Him, to the soul who seeks Him. It is good that one should hope and wait quietly for the salvation of the Lord."

-Lamentations 3:25-26

Personal moment: As a child, I had this great desire to drive a car. One so strong that I was always fascinated by the art of it all. I just could not wait to grow up, get my license and drive on my own. Taken by the idea of driving was I, that one time in my adolescent years I hopped in my father's parked truck at the time to simulate the act of driving. I played in the truck for a while until my curiosity would get the best of me. Apparently, just sitting in the truck was not good enough. I had the bright idea of playing with the gear shift until it came out of park! The truck then began to roll out of place, down a slight hill and straight into my grandfather's tool shed!

Though I was so expectant of driving way before my time, I was not expectant of the punishment and chastisement I received immediately afterwards. My expectancy of driving had taken me out of a child's place. My expectancy had also exceeded my maturity. Whenever your maturity does not match your expectancy, disastrous things can happen.

The Old Testament Prophet Jeremiah writes about having a spirit of expectation for the Lord. He says in Lamentations 3:25-26

"The Lord is good to those who wait for Him, to the soul who seeks Him. It is good that one should hope and wait quietly for the salvation of the Lord." He writes with an assurance that when we wait on God, good things are bound to come our way. He states that our spiritual expectation for God always yields a harvest. If our expectancy is in Him, the God we serve has a way of giving us just what we need.

In that same vein of waiting on the Lord or expecting Him to have His way in our lives I'm reminded of Isaiah 40:31. It reads "But those who wait on the Lord shall renew their strength; They shall mount up with wings like eagles, they shall run and not be weary, they shall walk and not faint."

When you are expectant for God to show up in your life, He not only shows up, but He brings strength, power and tenacity that you need to keep on moving. What are you expecting in life? Maybe you're expectant of a new position or for your family to come back together. Don't lose that hope. Pregnant women should not be the only ones in the world that are expectant. You too should be expecting just as I am. I'm expecting God to meet needs financially, emotionally, spiritually and physically.

Today's Declaration Challenge: Raise your level of expectation. Be mindful of the waiting process. It's a process that's sometimes long and frustrating but rewarding. Nothing worth having happened overnight. Let your expectation be towards God today. When your focus is on Him, He must meet your need. Let Him renew you. Your friends can't do that for you. Let Him give you the desires of your heart and not what man says you need. Today as you pray declare "God **I am expectant** of your will for my life.

Notes

I am expectant home &
husband. Must trust in the
Lord! Be patient & obidient.

Day 9

"I AM A MIRACLE"

"Immediately the fountain of her blood was dried up, and she felt in
her body that she was healed of the affliction."

-Mark 5:29

My twin brother and I were anticipated to be born in November of
1983. As things would turnout, we were born on September 22,
1983. If my brother Jerrell would tell it too he'd say, "Apparently,
you just couldn't wait to be born" (since I was born first) Ha! We
would face uncertain and rough days moving forward because we
were born two months early. We both were only a couple of pounds
and some ounces each. This subsequently led to us being
hospitalized for a while.

It is noteworthy that premature babies have an elevated risk
of early death and other conditions such as heart disease and mental
development issues. Personally, I'm sure my parents were aware of
the potential trouble we would face yet prayed for us, visited us often
and solicited prayers of the saints on our behalf that even our
outcome was not solid. Our mother had deemed us as her "miracle
babies." As time would have it, we would gain more weight and
eventually be released from the hospital. What a different scenario
from our start, when even our doctors were not completely hopeful.
God turned our lives around from not being able to breathe on our

own to fully functioning individuals. We had been the recipients of His miraculous power.

In the text before us today we see a woman who was also in need of a miracle. The scripture speaks of this woman with an issue of blood in such an odd way. Firstly, we don't even know this woman's name. We don't even know her background. We don't know if she had children or not. All that we know about her is her condition. We only know that she's suffering with a bleeding condition. Oh, how tragic her life must have felt to have been sick and broke. For we do know that she spent all her money on doctors and they could not help her. So not only was she sick but she was broke. Lord have mercy. This woman needed a miracle. I'm sure society and those around her probably wanted nothing else to do with her. In those times, persons that were sick were ostracized or cast away in society due to their illness.

When she heard that Jesus was passing by, she made a commitment to press her way to him. In desperation and a need for a miracle or change she made a connection to her problem solver. Mark 5:29 records that "Immediately the fountain of her blood was dried up and she felt in her body that she was healed of the affliction." Her faith and desire for better brought about her healing. Jesus told her "Daughter your faith has made you well. Go in peace and be healed of your affliction." (Mark 5:34).

Do you need a miracle today? Do you need a change in your reality? Some miracles may not be in the physical. Just a wave of extra money financially would be a miracle for that person that's broke. The mending of a broken family divided over things that happened 20 years ago can serve as a miracle. The calming of any great storm spiritually can be viewed as a miracle. Any suspension of natural law constitutes a miracle. My sisters and brothers I suggest to you that your miracle is in your faith.

What kind of faith do you have today? If it's little or no faith, then you're cancelling the propensity of your miracle. If you have faith in what seems impossible, God can exceed your imagination and make it possible.

Today's Declaration Challenge: I dare you to receive your miracle. You are a miracle. The fact that you've gone through all that you have, and you still have sanity, peace and love in your heart is a miracle. Today expect God to bring a miracle to your house. Your answer to prayers might be closer than you think. I challenge you to look for your turnaround today. Look for the very thing that others said you would not have. Declare today **"I am a miracle."**

Notes

My turnaround, Great Job.
Living independent
Buying my first home

Day 10

"I AM PRESERVED"

"And the Lord will deliver me from every evil work and preserve me for His heavenly kingdom. To Him be glory forever and ever Amen!"
-2 Timothy 4:18

I fondly remember growing up on the family farm as a child and watching my family harvest crops. From seeing my grandfather, father, and uncles prepare the gardens for seeds was interesting. Though I could have done without the heat, the process of putting the seed in the ground, watering them, fertilizing them and letting time take its course amazed me.

In the times of harvest, I noticed a thing happened next that was noteworthy. One of my aunts, Aunt Leola, would take the abundance or remaining portions that we did not consume and can it. Weeks and sometimes months later, the same okra, green beans, and soups would taste fresh out of the garden because they had been preserved.

Anybody that has ever gone to a grocery store has noticed preservatives near the sandwich aisle. Those ingredients have been sealed and kept in a manner that they don't lose their freshness. Once opened they become exposed to the elements and run the risk of losing their flavor. But if they are resealed and kept cool, the taste will last a long time.

Today I pray that God will preserve you in all things that you set out to do today. That's what all of us should desire for God to do within us. That's why you and I cannot quit this journey of life. That's why we can't give up on life based upon what we see. There's much work for you to do. The only way you will complete such a work is when you know that God will not only let you start a task but experience the anxieties in the middle of it and dance in relief as it comes to an end.

Now that you know that there's work for you to do, even your enemies can't stop you. Paul writes to Timothy about God's preserving power in 2 Timothy 4:18 "And the Lord will deliver me from every evil work and preserve me for His heavenly kingdom." Paul gives Timothy his hope of assurance of what God will do. He tells him that not only will God keep you from the enemy and adversary, but He will preserve you until heaven belongs to you. That person that's seasoned in years needs to know that God's keeping you alive to not only witness change but to also make heaven yours.

You may be wondering why God is keeping you in the position that you're in for as long as you've been in it. It's because God has graced you to handle that situation when others failed. He's preserved you to speak of your experience to others that may be going through what you've witnessed. You'll know that you're preserved because you won't even look like things you've been through.

Today's Declaration Challenge: I challenge you to reflect on the things that God has preserved you from. It may be a negative way of thinking or even people that were detrimental to your being. If you consider the fact that preservation belongs to you, you will carry yourself differently. You will find joy in the favor of God. I challenge you to share ways that God has preserved or kept you. Share your story with someone that needs to hear your testimony. Your words may uplift them from a state of despair. Today declare **"I am preserved."**

Notes

I dont look like what I gone through.

Day 11

"I AM REVIVED"

"Will you not revive us again, that your people may rejoice in You?"
- Psalm 85:6

As the clapping commenced, the songs went forth and the word of God was delivered and, in that moment, the "spirit of revival" was going on. Growing up in church, I looked forward to the revival season the most. Not for the fellowship with other churches but rather the opportunity for God to revitalize my spirit from the weariness that I had gathered from this world.

As a believer, you will experience days and moments where you need to be revived, revitalized and reignited with a zeal for life and even more, the things of God. There have been times in my existence where I needed an external push from someone to encourage me to go even further than I had already gone. You and I will experience so much even today and in coming days that will test our hearts and spirits on whether to endure or give up. When these things come against you, you too will stand in the need of a revival within.

The scripture for today is no different for those sons of Korah who penned it than how we feel today. Psalm 85:6 simply reads "Will you not revive us again, that Your people may rejoice in You?" The Sons of Korah pose this question to God himself, as they stand in need of a refreshing. They had undergone the process of falling short of God's glory. They knew what it was like to live a life of trouble. They as Israelites, had experienced their own sinful ways before God as a people. Even still he had received them back to himself. The Israelites were His. He restored them and their land, but they needed their hearts and spirits revived.

How could this be? How could anyone experience things around you come back together such as your family and finances, but you still need internal restoration yourself? Are you in that place today? I'm speaking of the place where you're comfortable in your resources and relationships, but you need to be revived personally? To answer that question, "YES" you could be well in your surroundings but still need internal peace. That's a matter of fact.

I submit to you today that God has a spirit of revival for you. When you are broken and at your wits end, you are a prime choice for God to restore you back to life. In Isaiah 57:15, God speaks through the prophet saying, "I will dwell in the high and holy place, with him who has a contrite and humble spirit, to revive the spirit of the humble, and to revive the heart of the contrite ones." That's good news today. If I bring my brokenness before Him and I get in His presence that He will revive me when I remain humble before Him. *Today's Declaration Challenge*: You may need revival in your finances, family and faith. You may need it internally due to letting someone else crush your spirit. Take a page from the Sons of Korah and cry out for your revival. Don't let it pass you by. I challenge you to never allow temporal things to set you back when God is trying to elevate you. Bring your emptiness to God. Let God fill you again. Could it be that you can't be filled due to something else taking the place of your faith? Remove from your mind that you cannot achieve greatness again. Live again. Declare today **"I am revived."**

Notes

I am revived; Revive me!

Day 12

"I AM AN INTERCESSOR"

"So the children of Israel said to Samuel, "Do not cease to cry out to the Lord our God for us, that He may save us from the hand of the Philistines."

-1 Samuel 7:8

May I pray for you? That question alone is one of the most selfless questions one could ever ask. I ask it because even though you may have prayed for yourself, your issues and current life dilemmas, there's even more solace and power we have when we pray for others also. It's the act of intercession.

Intercession, as it is defined by *Merriam-Webster* is "the act of interceding in prayer, petition or entreaty in favor of another." It's a characteristic you and I should always have. Be not deceived, we know how to pray for ourselves very well. Why is that? Well, I know what I'm up against physically, emotionally, spiritually and internally. I know how to tell God about myself in prayer. That's not difficult. On the flip side of that, I sometimes have a harder time praying for others if I don't make their problems real in my life. It's only when I put on the shoes of another, though they may not fit me properly or function well, but they help me to better understand the plight of another.

Throughout the Bible we see semblances of intercession at

work. In 1 Samuel 7:8 the children of Israel were amid an upcoming attack by the Philistines yet again. However, this time the circumstances were different because they did not have a good relationship with the Lord and chose to worship foreign gods. The Philistines wanted to seize the moment and attack, but the Israelites needed help. They called on Samuel to help them saying "Do not cease to cry out to the Lord our God for us, that He may save us from the hand of the Philistines." Samuel did just that. Verse 9 reads "Then Samuel cried out to the Lord for Israel and the Lord answered him." The passage would go on to show the Israelites beating the Philistines as God answered Samuel's prayer of intercession for Israel. What an awesome display of standing in the gap for another!

We see a similar occurrence in the New Testament as Peter found himself in prison as King Herod attacked those leaders in the early church. The text in Acts 12:5 reads "Peter was therefore kept in prison, but constant prayer was offered to God for him by the church." Because of them praying, an angel of the Lord would lead him out of prison. There's power in prayer. That's the kind of prayer I need. The type of prayer that changes things in separate locations. The kind that sends the right help when I need it the most.

We even see the Holy Spirit interceding for us as well. Romans 8:26 reads "Likewise the Spirit also helps in our weaknesses. For we do not know what we should pray for as we ought, but the Spirit Himself makes intercession for us with groanings which cannot be uttered." That's a blessed consolation to you and me today that even when our minds can't conceive the words to pray that the Spirit knows what to say for us.

What do you need the Spirit to intercede for you about? Could it be your family? Your acquaintances or maybe your career direction? It could be a prayer for protection or safety from harmful personalities. Let the prayers of the righteous help you.

Today's Declaration Challenge: Can you pray for those you meet today? Can you pray for that stranger that poured their heart out to you without even knowing you? Can you intercede for that enemy that once sought to take you out now that they are undergoing what they took you through? Will you pray for that soul that is easily offended at everything and never seeks to find their own strength? Do you need prayer? Seek out persons to pray for you that know the power and the worth of prayer. Today let your voice be heard by declaring **"I am an intercessor."**

Notes

Praying for my big brother and his family.

Day 13

"I AM WATCHFUL"

"But you be watchful in all things, endure afflictions, do the work of an evangelist, fulfill your ministry."

-2 Timothy 4:5

As a child growing up and serving at my home church, Fairfield UM Church, I often credit them for the training of a younger generation to serve God by working in the church. They put you to work. In addition to singing, another position that I enjoyed doing was serving as an usher at the doors of the house of the Lord. It gave me much fulfillment.

Ushers were the initial point of contact person for congregants as they entered church for worship. They passed out programs, lead persons to available seats, and assisted in the offering. They were the doorkeepers. Ushers had and have a certain presence about them that is vital to the workings of the church. They also had to be watchful in every area of the worship experience.

The idea of being watchful applies to our lives in many ways today. Honestly speaking, the more watchful that we are, the more aware and knowledgeable we are as well. It is a given fact that the more attentive to the things around us we are, the more prepared and equipped we are for changes as they happen.

The Apostle Paul writes to his mentee Timothy with a charge to his upcoming leadership in the early church as a preacher. He tells him "But you be watchful in all things, endure afflictions, do the work of an evangelist, fulfill your ministry" (2 Timothy 4:5). Paul charges him specifically to have his eyes open to his surroundings. For Paul, he wanted Timothy to see that if his eyes were open he could endure painful afflictions and carry out the work of ministry. No one can see dimly or with their eyes closed. Paul knew that sometimes in ministry and in life that you must see what you don't see. Sometimes you must look for what's on the inside of a thing or person to solve the problem.

What are you watchful of today? The things that have your attention the most, tend to rule your day. The people that you watch the most tend to shape your reality. The ones you speak to the most, tend to form your perspectives and opinions. Are you watching after your goals and dreams? Are you caught up in the things that are beneficial to you or the things that are detrimental? Are you watchful over your family just as you are your career?

Being committed to one thing over another does not mean you're a bad person. It means that the "one thing" may control the scope of your focus, your day and your time. The word for today speaks that we are called to be multifaceted to watch *all things*. In watching all things, yes, I will be stretched but I will also be mindful of many things. It makes me concerned for the complete ministry or family or connections and not just one part.

Today's Declaration Challenge: Today I challenge you to keep your eyes on all things. Just as that usher watches the doors and the concerns of the worshippers, so should your eyes be open. Just as the enemy watches for moments to overshadow us, we too should be watchful in combating evil with good. If Jesus told His disciples to "watch and pray" (Matthew 26:41), don't you think that we should also? Keeping your eyes open is not a sign of nosiness but rather a sign of awareness. For if I see the danger, I know what to pray for. If my eyes are fixed on the goals, dreams and issues that are before me, I'm not easily swayed on things that are behind me. I challenge you to keep your head up today and declare **"I am watchful."**

Notes

Eyes wide open at work
Eyes wide open with my family
Eyes wide open with my relationship
Be watchful!

Day 14

"I AM WONDERFULLY MADE"

"I will praise You, for I am fearfully and wonderfully made;
Marvelous are Your works, and that my soul knows very well."
-Psalm 139:14

You are truly one in a million. In fact, billions. Nobody else can be you in this world and that is your power. Your thoughts, your decisions and your genetic makeup are uniquely yours. Though you live in a world with billions with similar thoughts from time to time, you are the sole decider of the course of your life along the way.

In understanding the very wonderful way that you and I exist as individuals, I'm also impressed by the very intricate way that you and I have been made. Yes, it is true that you were born due to the brilliant conception of genes from our parents. Yes, we are the total of their personalities and mannerisms. The fact that you survived and persevered up until now shows that you were wonderfully designed. Creations that are considered works of art have stamps of approval on them. The maker or creator puts their seal and signature somewhere on them to identify that piece of art is theirs.

I submit to you today that God has done that thing for you and me. I believe that God has purposely made you and I to do mighty things. He has also ordered your steps today. I also believe that He has given you His seal of approval, by giving us His Son and His Spirit.

David recognized the creative genius of God. He had noticed his own life and all he had undergone. He reflects on himself and says "For you formed my inward parts; you covered me in my mother's womb. I will praise You for I am fearfully and wonderfully made" (Psalm 139:13-14a).

Even as king, David had an affinity and an appreciation for all that God had done for him. He recognizes that God knew all about him even as He formed him in his mother's womb. He understood that if God could do all of that for him, he owed God a praise. He makes a declaration that "I will praise You." He makes it personal. He lets his thankfulness be shown in praise. Let your praise be shown today. Don't let another praise God for you and your life better than you.

Today's Declaration Challenge: Can you thank God for how He made you? Are you still able to worship Him for putting your inward parts together? Who else but God can receive this praise? He made you so uniquely that every part of you works inwardly and outwardly to form a masterpiece. His seal of approval is on your life today. I challenge you to celebrate yourself today. Be thankful for your growth. Thank God for the maturity that you pushed yourself to. Never allow anyone to devalue the power you have. Never allow outside influences to negate you inside. Today declare **"I am wonderfully made."**

Notes

I am wonderfully made!
will Praise God & thank Him.

Day 15

"I AM COMFORTED"

"Blessed be the God and Father of our Lord Jesus Christ, the Father of mercies and God of all comfort, who comforts us in all our tribulation, that we may be able to comfort those who are in any trouble, with the comfort with which we ourselves are comforted by God."

-2 Corinthians 1:3-4

Growing up raising cattle and horses was indeed an experience to say the least. It was hard to not be attached to them. One horse that I ended up loving was one that we had by the name of "Queen." Everybody loved her. She was born on our land and so we all enjoyed watching her grow up.

Once she was broken in for riding and used to us, she was a joy to have. Like any animal, she had her way, but she was a great horse. One day while trying to get to other horses on our land, she jumped a barbed-wire fence and cut herself. She bled out and later passed away due to the injury. We were crushed. She was a part of the family. I remember we buried her on a hill on our land and my brothers and I had a little homegoing for her. We were in mourning. We sang and reflected on her life and in those moments, we were comforted.

For all of us have experienced loss of someone or something that we were really attached to. It was in those times that once the fact sunk in that our friend or family member was gone that we underwent some of the most hurtful moments of our lives. The very fact that a separation has occurred between loved ones will cripple you. Whether it be death, loss of a job or a property due to a tragic event, you will need comfort.

The Apostle Paul addresses the idea of being comforted. In 2 Corinthians 1:3-4 he states, "Blessed be the God and Father of our Lord Jesus Christ, the Father of mercies and God of all comfort, who comforts us in all our tribulation, that we may be able to comfort those who are in any trouble…" Paul gives honor and recognition to God as his comforter in distress. He goes on to let the church of Corinth know that we are comforted to give that same comfort back out to others.

Can you recall a time that God or even someone that was strong when you were weak comforted you? You may be in that place today where you need to be lifted. You may feel that you're stuck in a moment that's long gone where life as you knew it changed. Are you not allowing yourself to be healed and comforted from what happened? I suggest to you that *comfort* comes from God in many ways. It may be in a song (like it was for my brothers and I). It may be in a prayer by someone you know is strong at talking to God on your behalf. It may even be in the presence of friends or persons whom you've shared life's ups and downs with. It may be around your favorite laughing partner. Comfort may come in a memory of great times. However it comes, let it fill your heart. Let it ease your pain.

Today's Declaration Challenge: I challenge you to seek out comfort today from what has pained you. Let the spirit of God, the Comforter and Helper, overshadow you (John 15:26). Allow your heart to be healed. Even if you have experienced comfort in the past and you've healed from it, be bold enough to offer that same spirit of comfort to another. Your testimony, your smile and your witness may be just what someone else needs to turn their life around. If God did it for you, be strong enough to do it for your neighbor. Open your mouth and your heart and declare **"I am comforted."**

Notes

Gerald comforted me + my family when Roscoe passed away. I am healed.

Day 16

"I AM A BELIEVER"

"Jesus said to him, "Thomas, because you have seen Me, you have believed. Blessed are those who have not seen and yet have believed."

-John 20:29

My belief in God the Father, Jesus His Son and the Holy Spirit as my comforter, has been the anchor to my soul and faith. It is the core that makes me a believer. As a believer, I daily seek to use my words to shape my reality. My confession solidifies who I am and who I've found God to be in my life. Romans 10:9 reads that "if you confess with your mouth the Lord Jesus and believe in your heart that God raised Him from the dead, you will be saved." I speak it and therefore I believe it.

Who qualifies to call themselves believers? Are only the wealthy deemed to be believers? No. Are those who sit in places of power only believers? No. Are only those of a certain class or ethnicity believers? No. You and I are qualified as believers based on our acceptance of Jesus as the Lord of our lives.

By my confession, I affirm daily what I believe. Even in prayer, the act of me communicating to God keeps my line open to what I believe. One might pose a question and say, "How can you believe in a god that you don't see?" or "How do you claim to be blessed by a god you cannot touch?" Such was the case for the disciples upon seeing Jesus after His resurrection. He had been with them for three years of ministry, died and rose from the dead to their amazement. He already made an appearance to the disciples but one by the name of Thomas was absent. When the other disciples told him that they had seen the Lord, he chose to not believe unless he saw him for himself.

In Jesus' way of doing things, he later shows up 8 days later to the room that they were in and offered peace to them. He makes Thomas reach his hand on the piercings on His hand. He then challenges him saying "Do not be unbelieving, but believing. And Thomas answered and said to Him, My Lord and my God! Jesus said to him Thomas because you have seen Me, you have believed. Blessed are those who have not seen and yet have believed" (John 20:27-29).

What a unique blessing you and I have, to serve a Savior that we've never seen but we've felt His power in our hearts. But how many times do we wear the shoes of Thomas? How many times do we become like the father of the mute boy with seizures of Mark 9 who needed a miracle but had his doubts. He would tell Jesus "Lord I believe, help my unbelief." (Mark 9:24).

The issues of life will seek to make you disbelieve. Dealing with a sick loved one will sometimes cause you to question your faith. The loss of a resource or job will make your belief waiver. I've learned that one of the blessings of being a believer has nothing to do with your external but rather your internal foundation. True believers might face tragedies on the outside but feel nothing but triumph on the inside!

What do you believe today? Is your belief in the saving power of God? A strong belief system will anchor you from the ills of this world. Living off the belief of those that went before you is not enough. You must know what you know for yourself. You must seek after God for yourself. Do you believe that God can deliver, save and heal you from your issues? I believe that He can and that He can do it for you.

Today's Declaration Challenge: Believe in God again. I challenge you to believe that times will get better. Your trouble has an expiration date. Your storm winds will soon pass over. When you believe without seeing, it's not fiction but faith. I encourage you to look at your life through different lenses. Don't be unbelieving but rather believing that better belongs to you. Believe God for greater. Believe in your healing. Believe for your turnaround. Declare from your heart **"I am a believer."**

Notes

I believe he will make better days, I have come so far I know he wont forsake me. I am a believer!

Day 17

"I AM PERSUADED"

*"O Lord, You induced me, and I was persuaded; You are stronger
than I, and have prevailed."*

-Jeremiah 20:7a

I recall very well the moments in my younger life when I felt the call
to preach. It was like no other for me because I was given glimpses
of myself operating as a preacher in the form of dreams. On various
occasions, I would have the same dream of watching myself in a
pulpit bringing the message. It was the oddest thing. I couldn't
explain it, but I felt that God was pulling me into it. Every time I
tried to dismiss it, the same dream would occur or even while awake
God would put it on my mind and heart in a heavy way.

It would later happen that I was asked by youth leaders to
bring the message on our assigned youth day and the rest was
history. Though I was defiant about doing it, I believe
wholeheartedly that God softened my heart towards ministry. It was
not on my list of desires to do. By His love, grace and power, I was
persuaded to serve Him in a better way.

This idea of persuasion we even see in the Bible by today's
scriptural reference as the Prophet Jeremiah speaks. He has been
called by God and into the ministry as a prophet but has encountered
some struggles within that call. In Jeremiah 20:7 he says, "O Lord,
you induced me, and I was persuaded; You are stronger than I, and

57

have prevailed." He was distraught. Jeremiah no doubt felt that his ministry was in vain. The people that he was called to serve were not receptive of his efforts to turn back to God. He was being mocked by those around him and it was troubling him.

Have you ever felt like this? Have you ever felt drawn into something and persuaded into an arena you didn't desire to be in? How did it make you feel? You may be in that place today. Doing ministry and the things you love to do will at times make you feel unsuccessful. Things around you may have you feeling trapped and stretched at the same time. My friend, don't allow the opinions of others, who aren't productive themselves to belittle your calling and the work you've done. You're better than that.

Jeremiah was at an odd place. He was doing what God desired of him to do but did not feel like it. You will experience this too even on the right road. It's possible to do the right thing and feel ineffective. Don't allow what you're feeling to hinder what you're building. Jeremiah threatened to no longer speak on God's behalf anymore or even say His name. The only problem with that was that God's word was with him. In Jeremiah 20:9b he says, "But His word was in my heart like a burning fire shut up in my bones..." That's a sign of a heart that's fully persuaded towards God.

There will be things that will come up in the order of your day that will persuade you to be a part of it. You will be tempted to join in conversations for your input whether you want to or not. You will be put in things that were not on your radar to better help others and you must overcome your will for theirs. I've learned that some of the greatest things I've done were the ones I wasn't even thinking about, but God had others plans. Sometimes persuasion can be a blessing when it's guided in the right way.

Today's Declaration Challenge: I challenge you to not give up on the things that you have been called and even persuaded to. Sometimes familiar faces may mock you and doubt God's hand in your life, but continue. Prove the doubters wrong. You've got more in you than you realize. Allow God's word to rise in you today. Allow His hand to sustain you today even if you gave up yesterday. There's more life in you. There's more work in you. There's enough Word in you to endure any trouble. Proudly declare today **"I am persuaded."**

Notes

I am persuaded!

Day 18

"I AM SPIRITUAL"

"By this we know that we abide in Him, and He in us, because He has given us His Spirit."

-1 John 4:13

Every day that we live, we need the Spirit of God. There's no mistaking it. We absolutely need it to function. When we start the course of this day, we will undergo a gamut of things. Whether it be joy, sorrow, heartache, peace or immense success, these things make or break us internally and externally.

Since we are human beings, we have the propensity to operate in the flesh many times. This partiality to be fleshly can overwhelm who we are, that we have a demanding time understanding the things of God, the words of God and the ways of God. That's why Jesus told Nicodemus, "That which is born of the flesh is flesh, and that which is born of the Spirit is spirit. Do not marvel that I said to you, 'You must be born again" (John 3:6-7). This "new birth' creates a new life in you and I that is spiritual. However, to experience this new life we must be born again.

With that said, if I believe that I am spiritual, I daily wake up to change my character and my will for His will. That means I train and develop my thoughts to think from a spiritual perspective. This kind of perspective causes me to act according to His word and not according to my devices. This is not easy to do. Since its natural for me to act according to my will, I daily seek to reshape and make my actions emulate the actions of God through Jesus Christ. The "changing of the guard" from flesh to spirit is a tricky thing but a necessary thing. Having the Holy Spirit, will endow you with power. Acts 1:8 reads "But you shall receive power when the Holy Spirit has come upon you; and you shall be witnesses to Me in Jerusalem and in all Judea and Samaria, and to the end of the earth."

Throughout our lives we will encounter those that may not be where we are spiritually. There will even be those that may appear spiritual or knowledgeable about God but have not made Him their choice. We have a charge by the Apostle John concerning those we encounter from day to day. In 1 John 4:1-2 he states "Beloved do not believe every spirit, but test the spirits, whether they are of God; because many false prophets have gone out into the world. By this we know the Spirit of God: every spirit that confesses that Jesus Christ has come in the flesh is of God."

By keeping God first in our confession, we remain in the spirit of God. At some time, your spirit will be tried today. Those with "no spirit" always desire to extinguish the lights of those who do have it. It's inescapable. You have the power to control that narrative. You have the power to dismiss any spirit that is not like God's.

Today's Declaration Challenge: Today let spirit within you arise as you make sound decisions. Don't believe every spirit that comes your way today either. Some may have a spirit and it not be holy. I challenge you to even look for things that enhance the spirit of God in you. Things such as study groups, uplifting music and godly counsel from others that have made God their choice. By doing this, you set the stage for God to keep you in His will and in His way. Make your declaration that **"I am spiritual."**

Notes

I am spiritual!

Day 19

"I HAVE WISDOM"

"If any of you lacks wisdom, let him ask of God who gives to all liberally and without reproach and it will be given to him."
-James 1:5

My friends, not having wisdom can get you in an overabundance of troublesome situations. A person who is wise is careful in their thoughts, actions and words. Our natural tendency would be to speak and say the first thing that comes to mind. Though it may be honest, blunt and keeping it real, it may not be the best thing to say. Wisdom then makes us pause to give deference to strong counsel and truth.

Before anything successful is ever done or achieved, one must seek wisdom. Driving a car from one place to the next requires wisdom in watching traffic patterns, monitoring your speed and measuring the distance it takes to go anywhere in an allotted time. You need it even in food preparation. A cook or chef must be aware of the seasoning and temperature in order to not ruin the recipe. Wisdom must also be shown to be an effective communicator. A person must develop a great listening gift at what's being said and even not said to assess what they've heard and respond appropriately. It's unwise to hear someone speak about their pain in their body and bring up your favorite meal from last week. That's not only unwise but it's also rude.

The biblical book of wisdom is Proverbs. It's attributed to

King Solomon, the son of King David. He was the epitome of Israel's wisest of men. Therein this book, Solomon records many words of wisdom for everyday living. He states in Proverbs 24:3 about the makings of wisdom saying, "Through wisdom a house is built, and by understanding it is established; By knowledge the rooms are filled with all precious and pleasant riches." He paints the picture that if wisdom is not applied in what we do then we do it for nothing and to no gain. He also gives credence to learning and being informed and aware of anything that you would desire to do, prior to doing so.

Do you consider yourself to be wise? Do you have wisdom internally? To be taken seriously concerning anything great, you need it. If you feel that you're lacking wisdom James 1:5 reads "If any of you lacks wisdom, let him ask of God who gives to all liberally and without reproach and it will be given to him." He instructs that your search for wisdom lies in your request. When you truly long for it and ask God the Father for wisdom that He will supply it every time.

You may need wisdom to raise godly children in an ungodly world, ask the Father. You may be in the middle of a career change and need wisdom on whether to stay or go, ask God for it. Your responsibilities with your family and acquaintances may be pulling you from here to there and you want to meet every need, ask God for wisdom to cover every base and not feel drained in the end. Someone may be pushing your buttons today, but before you lose yourself, ask

God for wisdom to not react and redirect that negative energy into a positive. Just as Solomon asked for wisdom and gave out many of those same words to his descendants and those that came after him, you can do that for another.

Today's Declaration Challenge: I dare you to let **wisdom** rule the order of your day. When you are facing a giant that seemingly won't leave you, seek wisdom tools to overcome what's in front of you and not lose your position. Proverbs 4:5-7 says, "Get wisdom! Get understanding! Do not forget, nor turn away from the words of my mouth. Do not forsake her, and she will preserve you; Love her and she will keep you. Wisdom is the principal thing; Therefore, get wisdom. And in all your getting, get understanding." Wisdom and knowledge will help you, speak on your behalf and will preserve you. Today make a declaration that **"I have wisdom."**

Notes

I have wisdom. Asking God for wisdom in purchasing a home. Asking God for wisdom in going back to school.

Day 20

"I AM A WITNESS"

"You are my witnesses," says the Lord, And my servant whom I have chosen, that you may know and believe Me, and understand that I am He. Before Me there was no God formed, nor shall there be after Me."

-Isaiah 43:10

Let your witness be known today. Pray that God would grant you an opportunity to witness of His power and love for us to those you meet. The world we live in needs to know who you stand for. That's why in times like these we must pray that God grants us the courage and the moment to witness to others in His name.

I received a phone call once from a young brother that attended a church that I had preached at a few times. He had fallen on tough times and needed a word of encouragement. Instead of being dismissive, I listened to his concerns which were valid and just as real as any other person. I let him finish and then I informed him that daily he must command the power of his day and not be swayed by what he says. I told him that if God saved him and redeemed him that he would need to shift his thinking from fear to faith. He asked me to keep him and his family in prayer and I offered to pray on the line. He agreed, and I lifted him up in prayer by my witness of what God has done for me in the past.

None of that was stated for any selfish reasons, but to show the overall importance that the world needs our witness. It does us no good as believers to attend church on Sundays and midweek services, to hear, applaud and praise from great sermons but leave the worship experience and not share all that word to someone else in their time of need. We then become like "full sponges" that can absorb things around but refuse to release them to those we encounter.

The Prophet Isaiah spoke on the Lord's behalf in Isaiah 43:10 when he states, "You are my witnesses," says the Lord, And My servant whom I have chosen, that you may know and believe Me, and understand that I am He. Before Me there was no God formed, nor shall there be after Me." Here we see God taking ownership over us who believe in Him and empowering us to know that we are His. We are His voices. We are the vessels that God desires as His representatives in the earth. If we fail to acknowledge Him and boost other gods before Him, we then make ourselves out to be deceived. We also cancel the possibility of letting God's power be operative in our lives.

We live in a time where the methodology of witnessing may have changed in some ways, but I believe it still has much weight in the uplifting of God's Kingdom. Those who believe used to go on door to door missions passing out ministry tracks and praying with those that so desired it. Society and technology would shift this practice to where now that form of witnessing is not as common. With the rise of technology and the speed of electronic information, we now see witnessing happen on social media platforms in great lengths to reach the generations of today. We know Romans 10:17 is clear when it says, "So then faith comes by hearing and hearing by the word of God." No matter the method, we have a mandate to share the joy of the Lord that we carry within us to others that we meet.

How strong is your witness? Are your ears attentive to the cries of others around you or are they muted to only hear your own internal reasoning? When we think about the potential ministry moment for God to uplift a person by our presence and words of comfort it should give us hope. That alone should cause us to always be looking, listening and excited about telling someone about the God who saved, forgave and redeemed us to live for Him.

Today's Declaration Challenge: Just as Ananias charged and spoke into Saul, the former persecutor of Christians after his Damascus Road experience where God had to blind him, save him and change his life, you too can do that for someone. You don't have to tell your life story. You don't have to share all your business in a ministry moment but simply be real and available. Just let your heart and love for God be shown and declare **"I am a witness."**

Notes

I am a witness!
Pay attention of the cries
of others.

Day 21

"I AM NEVER ALONE"

"Have I not commanded you? Be strong and of good courage; do not be afraid, nor be dismayed, for the Lord your God is with you wherever you go."

-Joshua 1:9

Your life matters. Your life has value and meaning. There is purpose on the inside of you. As you arose today and began doing the things you were obligated to do or desired to, you will find that at times you will be alone. The fact that you do many things alone, does not make you lonely.

As an individual, I enjoy my own company. I take pleasure in the moments of solitude and I try to use those moments for reflection and restoration. Society and different peer circles will try to dictate to you that you need someone by your side to be whole or complete. In my opinion that is incorrect. You were made and born whole, and another person will not determine that. The benefit is that another person will compliment who you are and bring added value and favor to you.

I suggest to you today that since your life matters, God desires for you to do exceptional things alone. Did you say alone? Yes, I said alone. There are moments that I believe God calls you and I to become leaders and set apart from the pack to do what we otherwise would have shied away from. Such was the case with

Joshua in the times of Moses and the Israelites. Joshua had served with Moses over the army of Israel. Moses led from the spiritual and prophetic perspective while Joshua led the military endeavors. At the time of this text Moses had just died and the people needed a leader. God speaks directly to Joshua and instructs him on keeping the law in his mouth as he leads the people. He then tells him in Joshua 1:9 "Have I not commanded you? Be strong and of good courage; do not be afraid nor be dismayed, for the Lord your God is with you wherever you go." What a great word of assurance!

As a believer, there are times that God sets the stage for you to soar and become who you've desired and other times he makes you pursue great feats without your permission. There are moments that your greatness must be shown, and it can't be shown hidden in the crowd. However it happens, you must find a courage that you may not have had and let God lead the way. Stepping out is never easy. Serving alone is never easy but the blessing in it all is that God gave a promise to Joshua in chapter 1:5 that "I will not leave you nor forsake you."

Jesus had to make a similar promise to His disciples. They had learned from him for three years and after his resurrection he had to return to His Father in heaven. He tells them in Matthew 28:20 "lo I am with you always, even to the end of the age. Amen." That's a comfort that cannot be described that every time you stand to do whatever God has purposed in your heart to do that He'll be with you. If you ever stand up without Him, then you're in for a different kind of help. As you go through school, work and your extracurricular activities know that though you can't see Him (God) know that He's always there.

Today's Declaration Challenge: In your quiet moments, let God strengthen you. I challenge to maximize the time alone to better yourself. Study your craft. Find your own joy and peace. Enjoy your own company. Take yourself out to eat. Kick back and take in a movie. Celebrate your own progress. Stand out. Serve God and His people humbly and look yourself in the mirror and say to yourself **"I am never alone."**

Notes

I am never alone, but when I am by myself I enjoy my own company.

Day 22

"I AM TRANSFORMED"

"And do not be conformed to this world, but be transformed by the renewing of your mind, that you may prove what is that good and acceptable and perfect will of God."

-Romans 12:2

Every day that we live we should be able to see the transformation within ourselves of who we've grown to be. It should be ongoing. It is a matter of fact that you are not the same person that you were 20 years ago, 10 years ago and even 5 days ago. The one thing that is constant in this world is change. You and I should always be able to view ways inwardly that we are transforming to our best selves.

I submit to you today that it's not what happens to you externally that changes you but rather what happens internally. When you decide internally that better belongs to you then you won't stop until you see it manifest. That calls for a change in the current way of doing things to give way to a new order.

The Apostle Paul writes to the Roman believers in exhortation and encouragement in the text before us. He serves notice to them in a way to be vigilant in their walk. He identifies that the world that they were in could easily sway anyone away from living a life after God's heart. He says, "Do not be conformed to this world but be transformed by the renewing of your mind..." (Romans 12:2). Paul speaks here with transformation in mind. He comes from the perspective that a person of faith is different than a person of the world. By conforming to the world's system or order of doing things, we are no longer set apart or distinguishable as a believer. He later gives them directives that if we have a renewed mind, that we made valid or true the will of God for our lives in our transformation.

God's will for you today and every day is for you to evolve and become greater than you are right now. Do you feel transformed since the Lord came into your life? Have you received a renewed mind? Are you in your own way from receiving a true transformation? There's more inside of you. Change will happen if it is welcomed. Maturity will take residence if it is invited.

I remember the cartoon "Transformers" had the theme song that stated that they were "more than meets the eye." Can you say the same? Is there more to you than what people see? Paul would write to the Galatians that "I have been crucified with Christ; it is no longer I who live but Christ lives in me; and the life which I now live in the flesh I live by faith in the Son of God. (Galatians 2:20)."

My friend, having Christ within brings about a transformation. You're no longer the same. He's transformed the parts in you that you thought would never change. Was it an overnight change? No it was not. There's levels to this. I'd rather grow with God than suffer without Him. I'd rather be different than remain the same any day.

Today's Declaration Challenge: In what way have you been transformed? How have you grown? Allow the spirit of being transformed to be your portion today. I challenge you to position yourself to be unlike the world and its ideals. We have enough copycats. Thank God for the process of changing. Take hope in the promise that a changed mind produces a changed life. Check your connections today. If your associates are still trapped in 10 years ago and refuse to transform to a better way of living and doing things, then maybe you've outgrown them. It's okay to call people to a higher standard. Wherever you may be today lift your head and declare **"I am transformed."**

Notes

I am transformed. I have matured
God lives within me.

Day 23

"I AM POWERFUL"

"Then He called His twelve disciples together and gave them power and authority over all demons and to cure diseases."
-Luke 9:1

Do you have power? If your answer is Yes, then where did you get it from? Power is defined by *Merriam-Webster* as "the ability to act or produce an effect, or possession of control, authority or influence over others. Again I ask Do you have power?

I can remember being in a department store parking lot years ago trying to get home and my car would not start. No matter what I did it was not working. I just knew that it was the battery. I got a replacement battery and went on my way. Well as things would happen, the car began to act up again and not start up. I called my father to assist me. He came and upon review he discovered that though the new battery was in place it had become disconnected from the cables that kept it in place. Hence no power was flowing. We reconnected it and tightened it and the car started with no hang-ups. When you're connected to the right source, you have power that is indescribable.

Such is the case for Jesus' disciples in the text for today. He intentionally gathered them together and gave them power to handle those they would encounter on their journeys. Luke 9:1 reads "Then He called His disciples together and gave them power and authority over all demons, and to cure diseases. He sent them to preach the Kingdom of God and to heal the sick." Jesus knew that they would need His power and authority to be effective.

In every setting you find yourself in today, let God's power guide your thoughts, movements and activities. You may be facing some demons of your own that were sent to derail you from your assignment but by the power vested in you, you can cast them out. Send them on their way and carry on. Whatever you do, don't allow anything that's not like God to set you back. Let God's power enable you to heal torn relationships with family and friends you thought you'd not speak to again. The power of God within you will fortify you for your next place. It will settle you and prepare you to be around gloomy people and still find joy.

Today when life gets heavy, allow the Spirit of God to help you find your power. Luke 24:49 reads that Jesus said, "Behold I send the Promise of my Father upon you; but tarry in the city of Jerusalem until you are endued with power from on high." Even at your weakest moments, God will look out for you. The promise of His Spirit will hold you together until your power comes back. God's power will allow you to finish what you started and see the end of a thing even when you wanted to give up in the middle.

Today's Declaration Challenge: Operate in God's power today. It's His power that has brought you this far anyway. By giving yourself over to God's power you will find that you're stronger than you realize. You have power to change communities. You have the power to uplift the broken. You have the power to heal those bound by sickness in prayer. I encourage you to change the game. Set the stage for God's power to show up and show out through you. When His power operates in you, people will know the difference. Let his Spirit uphold you when you're weak and endow you to proudly declare **"I am powerful."**

Notes

_____

_____

_____

_____

_____

_____

Day 24

"I AM A SOWER"

"Do not be deceived, God is not mocked; for whatever a man sows, that he will also reap."

-Galatians 6:7

I firmly believe in the blessing of sowing. Even though I saw this firsthand as a child growing up on a farm, I didn't fully grasp the totality of this concept until I became older. Honestly speaking there are many things that we don't attain until our level of maturity can receive it.

The concept or notion of being a sower is one that must be instructed and engrafted in the sower. Why is that? Because it's hard for some people to understand sowing when they are only looking forward to reaping. We as a people are naturally reapers. Reapers are very identifiable. Reapers typically receive what is planted but those who are sowers are the ones who release the seeds to be planted. There is a sacrificial component to sowing. It calls for one to give of themselves in hopes that their giving is not in vain.

Parents and caregivers are sowers. They are because they have an opportunity to sow into their child from birth until adulthood and beyond. They have the priceless privilege of molding ideas and thoughts into their child's mind that ultimately shapes their reality. Entrepreneurs and business owners sacrifice who they are, their time and their energy to cultivate a successful business that they love dearly. Pastors, spiritual leaders and churches have a unique opportunity as well to sow and create a culture that is Christ centered and fruitful in the communities that they serve. These examples exude sowing one to another with an expectation of a return on their investment.

Understand this, the seed is always smaller than the harvest. Zechariah 4:10 instructs us to "not despise the day of small beginnings, for the Lord rejoices to see the work begin." The return of that small seed is unmeasurable when it has come to fruition. I challenge you as a parent, grandparent, guardian or family friend to not give up on that child that's wayward at times before they have reached their fullest potential. If you give up on the seed, you will forfeit the blessing of the harvest.

Paul tells the churches of Galatia "Do not be deceived, God is not mocked; for whatever a man sows that he will also reap. For he who sows to his flesh shall reap corruption, but he who sows to the Spirit will of the Spirit reap everlasting life" (Galatians 6:7-8). It's a simple principle but profound at the same time. If you sow goodness and important things into others, it comes back and yields a dynamic blessing on your behalf.

No matter how rough or even how well things may be going for you today, you have a responsibility to watch what you sow. That means you and I must watch our words because if we always sow negatively then that will eventually be what we reap. If positivity is shown to others, it comes back around to you in due time. The hardest part in sowing is waiting for the manifestation. If you've invested time, love and peace in that person or situation, let God give the increase and the harvest in His own time.

Today's Declaration Challenge: What are you sowing? Are you the voice of dissension in your circle or one of encouragement? When was the last time you gave into someone else's future? I challenge you to pray for persons to sow into. Sow into something or someone that even may not be able to do the same for you. It's still better to give than to receive. I'd rather give or sow joy when my neighbor needs it the most than to be waiting for it to be done to me. Declare today **"I am a sower."**

Notes

_____

_____

_____

_____

_____

_____

_____

Day 25

"I AM ABUNDANTLY LIVING"

"The thief does not come except to steal, and to kill and to destroy. I have come that they may have life and that they may have it more abundantly."

-John 10:10

My prayer for you today is not that you just live but you live abundantly. If you're like me, you take care of your normal obligations and then try to enjoy the remaining moments of your day in peace. Sometimes after all that your heart and spirit is spent and weary. You then wake to do it all over again the next day and the day after. Whether today is one of those days that you feel drained or not, I want you to know God desires for you to live not only your best life but a life of abundance.

What does an abundant life look like? Is it a life free from trouble or maybe one that is full of earthly possessions and acquaintances? I beg to differ. I don't believe God gave us this opportunity of life for us to squander it on things that will fade away and fall apart. I don't believe that an abundant life is one that is only filled with many friends of influence either. I personally believe that an abundant life is one that has God the Father leading you, Jesus, His Son as a Savior and the Holy Spirit as a comfort. I believe that a life of abundance is one that exists under the banner that *"I'm living to live again."*

In the scripture reference today, Jesus speaks to His disciples and tells them in John 10:10 that "The thief does not come except to steal, kill and to destroy. I have come that you may have life and that you may have it more abundantly." He puts the word out there to them that there are people designated as thieves and robbers to try their best to take what is yours as if it's theirs. There are persons in this world that will do whatever they can to rob you of enjoying the fruit of this life. They will speak ill of you and try their best to pull you down to their level. Due to their own insecurities, they cannot fathom anyone else being successful. Don't stoop to their level. You've worked too hard to do that.

Jesus even challenged his disciples' way of thinking to know that there is more to life than what we see. In Luke 12:23 he says, "Life is more than food, and the body is more than clothing." Today I'm believing God with you for whatever you always desired to do but lacked the moment to do it. I encourage by the power of God's word to not let the routine of normalcy cause you to miss the newness of your future. If you can see yourself doing the impossible, by faith it will come to pass. If you can see beyond right now, the perspective of your life will change. Abundant living consists of going after that thing you talked yourself out of from fear of failure.

"With God all things are possible (Matthew 19:26) and if you see things as you've always seen them, you limit the power of God. I implore you to view things as God would. Live life not out of fear but by faith. When you operate under faith and the Christ as the center of life, your goals become attainable.

What does abundant life look like to you? Is it a life that completes what they start or one that gives up on the finish line due to a rocky middle? Are you living an abundant life? Do you desire for more than this current moment? If you do you, you are already setting the stage for God to do wonders on your behalf. An abundant life is a life that is forward thinking and not bound by the actions of others.

Today's Declaration Challenge: I challenge you to go after that thing that you put on the back-burner years ago. Live your best life. Make attainable goals. Shift your thinking from here to there. Take small steps to go on that trip you've always talked about. Be wise enough to dismiss any thief that comes to steal, kill or destroy you from your rightful place. You cannot live an abundant life with leeches attached to your destiny. Make the rest of your days the best of your days and declare **"I am abundantly living."**

Notes

Start saving money
Enroll into school
Look into different degrees

Day 26

"I AM A LEADER"

"Now therefore, go, lead the people to the place of which I have spoken to you. Behold, My Angel shall go before you."
-Exodus 32:34

You are a leader whether you realize it or not. Real leaders can lead even if they're not recognized in front of others. Leadership is a quality that we all possess even if it's not always identified by us. If you serve as a leader in your profession, you do so with the mentality that you have sharp vision and executive skills to be the conductor of daily operations not only for yourself and everyone that submits under you.

As a leader many times you must wear hats that you otherwise would not. You must sacrifice time and your own desires many times for the greater good and so that the group or project that you lead will progress successfully. When you're able to do that, you lead with a goal in mind and finish line in view.

What makes a leader great? Is there appearance or their posture? I would dare say that it's their posture and their heart for what they do. Leaders lead out of love, wisdom and transparency. We see such in the life of Moses in the text before us today. He had led the Israelites out of Egyptian captivity and they were on their way to the land of promise. Due to their obedience, the Israelites began to worship a golden image instead of worshipping God. This troubled Moses to see their sin. He questioned their motives, and some came back to the Lord's side. He went on to ask the Lord to forgive their sin. The Lord speaks to Moses concerning the people and Moses' job in Exodus 32:33-34 saying "Whoever has sinned against Me, I will blot him out of My book. Now therefore, go lead the people to the place of which I have spoken to you. Behold My Angel shall go before you. Nevertheless, in the day when I visit for punishment, I will visit punishment upon them for their sin."

As a leader you will have rough moments. They are inevitable. You will have times that those you lead will turn their backs to the word you bring and the set order for the group. You will have moments where even you will question your abilities. The weight of the call will sometimes be heavy but keep leading. Moses' role was to lead them to the Promised Land but, yet he let his own anger get in the way. The Lord reminded Moses that if you do what I've told you to do, I will handle those that dwell in sin and not the promise.

When was the last time you led anyone? It may have been a young family member coming after you in an endeavor that you mastered years ago. It could have been in leading a group of friends in your favorite activity. Was your leadership style received well? If not, why not? Was it clear as to what exactly you were doing as a leader? Could those you were leading tell that you did so out of a genuine heart? People are more prone to follow leaders that they can understand and grab the vision of that leader. Being a leader, will not make everyone like you. You will be despised and talked about and lied on. Lead not by emotions or familiarity, but out of a higher calling and assignment to fulfill.

Today's Declaration Challenge: Luke 6:39 reads "Can the blind lead the blind? Will they not both fall into the ditch?" As you lead in whatever capacity God has given you, do it out of a love for it. Lead out of a desire to see your project, ministry or business flourish. Lead with open eyes, ears and hearts. I also challenge you to invest in your role as a leader. Take time for yourself and your betterment. Be encouraged to know that your efforts are not worthless. Reflect on all the notable examples of leaders that went before you and let each enlighten your heart on how to be strong at what you do. I pray the spirit of longevity over you. With your eyes fixed on God, you will not go astray. Let your declaration be known today **"I am a leader."**

Notes

Leader @ work, try to see the finish line. I lead with love and respect, but also must get those back on track that fell astray.

Day 27

"I AM PATIENT"

"But let patience have its perfect work, that you may be perfect and complete, lacking nothing."

-James 1:4

One of the hardest things for anyone to have is patience. It's mentioned over 30 times in the Bible for a reason. One of the toughest times to have patience is when you're traveling. I recall going to Las Vegas for an event. As I was making my way to the airport, I got there moments before my plane was set to take off. As I made it to the gate, the airport crew closed the door! I was done. I missed my flight and I thought I would fall apart (ha).

Of course as I went to the counter to try and get on, the attendant though she was nice, refused to let me on. I then asked about future flights leaving the airport and to my shock it would be many hours later. I sucked it up and got my new ticket for a much later flight and right about that time a lady came by in a same plight as me. She was to be on the same plan. We ended up speaking about the matter and come to find out we had a lot in common.

She had a little dog and, so we played with the dog for a bit and took turns looking out for any news at our new gate. Once time had passed it was nearly the next day. We made the flight to Vegas and said our goodbyes. Though my impatience almost got the best of me, having someone in a same boat with me allowed me to handle the wait and the process much better.

James writes the text of today to give us a better understanding of patience in our lives. In James 1:4 "But let patience have its perfect work that you may be perfect and complete, lacking nothing." He suggests that patience must work on us. The idea of it having a perfect work means a "mature" work in us. Patience must rise to a certain level of maturity for us in life. There will be times that we will not be able to bear the process of waiting but the result is well worth it.

How is your patience? Do you consider yourself to have much of it? What in your life are you patiently waiting for? Are you waiting for a change in your resources or place of employment and your patience is running thin? Don't let your impatience cause you to forfeit the blessing of favor that God desires to give you. What has been a blessing for me in understanding patience is that God himself has been patient with me in my life many times until I got myself together and so why can't I do the same.

Today's Declaration Challenge: I challenge you to seek after more patience today. Patience with your kids, parents, siblings and coworkers. People are going through battles that you may never hear them say but if you would allow maturity to prevail, you will save yourself a lot of repercussions down the road. James 5:8 reads "You also be patient. Establish your hearts, for the coming of the Lord is at hand." In your patience, the harvest that is destined for you will be complete. In your impatience, that same blessing won't be done. I challenge you to wait for what God has for you and declare **"I am patient."**

Notes

_____

_____

_____

_____

_____

_____

_____

Day 28

"I AM HOPEFUL"

"Now may the God of hope fill you with all joy and peace in believing, that you may abound in hope by the power of the Holy Spirit."

-Romans 15:13

Where does your hope lie today? When you go throughout the day one can tell where your hope comes from by our actions. Many people have occupied their lives with things and activities to give them hope. My hope comes from God.

I have the assurance of hoping in Him because He enables me to see the good even in the face of bad. For me, my family members, even those that have gone on, had a firm hope in the power of God and what He could do in our lives if we let Him. Having hope in God does not make us foolish but it secures our spirits in our futures that no matter what comes our way, from God we will not stray.

Paul speaks on this very thing when he tells the Romans in Romans 15:13 "Now may the God of hope fill you with all joy and peace in believing, that you may abound in hope by the power of the Holy Spirit." Believing in God will give you a hope when you need it the most. Being hopeful gives you something to long for. It gives you goals that others may not have. It makes the difference in your life.

We live in a time when people place their hope in possessions and their careers before they will place it in God. We cast no judgment on them, but in retrospect the things we have today we could lose them tomorrow. We know that faith is the substance of things *hoped* for and the evidence of things not seen (Hebrews 11:1). Since we are a people of faith, we must allow our faith and hope to settle us in an uncertain world.

You may be hoping for God to open a door that you've been pursuing for quite some time. Let that hope come alive in you. You may be hoping that God repairs your friendships to a place of cordiality, but you must trust and hope in His plan. When you have hope, you have a peace that everything will fall into place.

Today's Declaration Challenge: I challenge to do as King David when he said in Psalm 39:7 "And now Lord what do I wait for? My hope is in You." Find hope in God today. In your distress, gather yourself and seek the hope that only God can give. I challenge you to have hope for your family. Hope will let you see yourself better before it happens. Declare today **"I am hopeful."**

Notes

_____

_____

_____

_____

_____

_____

_____

Day 29

"I AM GIFTED"

"Therefore I remind you to stir up the gift of God which is in you
through the laying on of my hands."

-2 Timothy 1:6

To see a person operating in their gifting is amazing. It is awesome
to witness because you can easily tell that they are called to the thing
that they are doing. They do it without hesitation. It's a natural thing.
I'm often astonished when children can pick up musical abilities
before they can even read better than grown-ups who struggle with
lessons. When you operate in your gift it's a beautiful thing.

My brothers, cousins and I were singing from early on in our
childhoods. It came as a joy to us. Even now we're mostly still
involved with music into our adult lives. You can't run too far from
the gift that is purposed for you. It may be musical, athletics,
cooking, life coaching or being a helper to others in their time of
need. One thing that I've learned is the same people can do the
operate in the same gift but be completely different. That's why I can
sing a song one way and my twin brother can sing it a separate way.
Therein lies the authenticity of a gift.

The Apostle Paul speaks to his young mentee Timothy in the
scripture reference for today about this very thing. He has spent
much time pouring life into him to prepare him for ministry. He tells
him in 2 Timothy 1:6 "Therefore I remind you to stir up the gift of

God which is in you through the laying on of my hands." The idea of stirring it up is a sign that Timothy may not have been using all that God had blessed him with. One might surmise that he was hesitant due to fear because the very next verse says, "For God has not given us a spirit of fear, but of power and of love and of a sound mind" (2 Timothy 1:7). Fear will keep you still in a place of doing nothing when God has blessed you with all that is needed to get the job done.

I submit to you today whether you're young or older to not let anyone talk you out of using the gift that God has given you. People with no gifting love to tell those who are gifted what to do and when to do it. Don't let the spirit of fear or intimidation keep you from exercising your gift. Be mindful that you can't run from what God has given you nor can you give it back. "For the gifts and the calling of God are irrevocable" (Romans 11:29).

Today's Declaration Challenge: Are you using all your gifts? I mean really using them? I challenge you today to use your gift as God gives you the opportunity. If he entrusted you with it, He knows the magnitude of how effective you are and the people you will touch as you use it. Practice does make perfect. It also prunes you and molds to be solid in your foundational abilities within your gift. I challenge you to never lessen your gift due to another's inability to receive it. Let your declaration be known that **"I am gifted."**

Notes

I am gifted in many things
Stir it up.

Day 30

"I AM PRODUCTIVE"

"For a good tree does not bear bad fruit, nor does a bad tree bear good fruit. For every tree is known by its own fruit. For men do not gather figs from thorns, nor do they gather grapes from a bramble bush."

-Luke 6:43-44

What are you producing? What have you already produced? What do you desire to produce? The idea of producing something should be ideal in the life of each of us. I firmly believe that when this life is over that I want to finish on "complete" and not "in progress." That should be your desire as well.

We all can readily agree that there were some things in life that we started but did not finish. It might be a half-painted room (ha) or a project that we gave up on because the image in the middle didn't look like the end. We've all been there. Someone may be there right now. I encourage you to know that no matter how you start or even how many times you start it, what matters is that you finish.

Jesus poses such an idea to His disciples about bearing or producing fruit. In Luke 6:43 He says, "For a good tree does not bear bad fruit, nor does a bad tree bear good fruit." He makes it known that if good trees thrive and do well, that they produce good fruit. It's inevitable. A bad tree cannot produce good fruit. We are productive by the sum of our nature. Jesus also stated in Matthew 7:20

"Therefore by their fruits you will know them." Our fruits make us essentially who we are.

If all I produce is negativity then you would not want any of my fruit because what good could it bring. If the words that I say about myself are self-defeating, then by what means will I ever become successful. I then disqualify myself from ever seeing the finish line to my progress. Be leery of those that will talk themselves out of their harvest. I don't know about you, but I need my harvest. I need my labor and I need my reward.

Today's Declaration Challenge: While you're going through this day, go back to the thing that you only gave 30% of yourself to. The other 70% of you will show up and bless you indeed. A productive life is a prosperous life. Are you producing your God-ordained or given fruit? Are you letting yesterday's limits help you with today's goals to finish tomorrow's test? You can produce greatness. I often say greatness can come out of a great mess. Turn your situation around. Put your time in. Let your fruit speak for you. Declare wholeheartedly **"I am productive."**

Notes

Day 31

"I AM FRIENDLY"

"A man who has friends must himself be friendly, But there is a friend who sticks closer than a brother."

-Proverbs 18:24

In this life, if you have genuine friends you must truly treasure them. There are very few persons that will attach themselves to your lives and remain throughout every season. Why is that? Well things often change around us. Situations change, and people change sequentially.

With that said, would you be who you are without all the persons in life that you've called a friend? For many, that answer would be a resounding no because our friendships ultimately make us or break us. Right now you know that there are some people from years gone by that may not be in your circle now, that really were influential parts of your being in that time. Even now, there are persons that you have not known that long who are and have become crucial assets to your life.

On the flip side of that, there are others that may not have been beneficial to you that were in your life, but you still learned what not to do from being in their midst. I suggest to you that some friends will be with you in your time of need as you would do the same for them. These same persons would even testify that your life adds value to theirs and vice versa. Mutual connections such as that are to be honored.

In the word reference for today, Solomon speaks about friendships saying, "A man who has friends must himself be friendly, but there is a friend who sticks closer than a brother." He serves notice that if you want friends, that you simply need to be friendly. No one has ever gained friends in rudeness or condescension. That profits you nothing. A great friend can be even better than a blood brother or sister.

Are you friendly? As you go to school and sit at your desk at work, can your associates see a friendly nature in you? Is your disposition amicable? You do know that you have the power to receive friends or shun them. Your blessings are not always tied to how people treat you but rather sometimes how you treat them.

Jesus would even share with his disciples in John 15:14-15 "You are My friends if you do whatever I command you. No longer do I call you servants, for a servant does not know what his master is doing; but I have called you friends, for all things that I heard from My Father I have made known to you." For you and me to be called friends of God should be our longing. Of course the opposite of such would be when we make ourselves friends with the world. James 4:4b reads "Whoever therefore wants to be a friend of the world makes himself an enemy of God." That goes without saying that I don't need that in my life.

Today's Declaration Challenge: I challenge you to make yourself friendly today to at least one person. You don't have to tell them your life's story but simply show respect to them. Show grace to them. Show a smile to them. Show God to them. In doing so, your efforts will lift them up. We are many times just one connection away from a totally different life. I challenge you to serve others as Christ and watch your status change from servant to friend. Go outside of your norm and declare today **"I am friendly."**

Notes

_____

_____

_____

_____

_____

_____

_____

Day 32

"I AM KINGDOM-MINDED"

"But seek first the kingdom of God and His righteousness, and all these things shall be added to you."

-Matthew 6:33

What's on your mind? Are you bogged down with the issues of this world? Maybe you're still caught up on something that happened 10 years ago and it's now ruling your present reality. Are you more mindful of the ways of others more than the ways of God? Whatever is on or in your mind controls you.

Today as things are moving along, my prayer is that you desire to have a "kingdom mind" within. One might ask what does that consist of? I surmise that a kingdom mind is one that is purposed to honor the things of God above the things of this world. It's a mind that's focused seeing others come into the knowledge of who God the Father is and the workings of His kingdom.

Jesus sets the stage for one to understand the importance of being mindful of the kingdom of God. In Matthew 6:33 He states, "But seek first the kingdom of God and His righteousness, and all these things shall be added to you." While many times we are concerned and focused on the earthly things of this world such as social groups, careers and family issues, when we have another obligation. As believers and those that profess a called-out life by God, we firstly should always be focused on the kingdom.

That means when we arise in the morning, our priority should be to communicate with God our appreciation for letting us see another day. We should also seek His will for our lives to guide our footsteps and help us discern what we should do. By doing this we allow His kingdom to come and reign over us. In knowing His will for you sets the platform for God to operate in your life. Jesus tells His disciples in Matthew 13:11 when asked why he spoke in parables that "Because it has been given to you to know the mysteries (hidden truths) of the kingdom of heaven, but to them it has not been given. The character of kingdom-minded persons is different than others because God reveals truths to you that others don't have.

It's hard to be kingdom minded if you're thinking is not forward bound but rather backwards. Luke 9:62 reads "But Jesus said to him, "No one having put his hand to the plow and looking back is fit for the kingdom of God." In other words, kingdom-minded people are always looking ahead for what's next. They are not bound to silly issues of times long past. They are goal oriented. They're so focused on what's next that even their character is separate from the rest. They understand what Galatians 5:21 says when it reads "envy, murders, drunkenness, revelries, and the like; of which I tell you beforehand, just as I also told you in time past, that those who practice such things will not inherit the kingdom of God."

I'm living to see the kingdom. That's the goal of a kingdom minded person. Your prayer today should be the same. Being mindful of that, brings you to a place of elevated thinking. When was the last time you thought in a manner of the kingdom? Go get your inheritance.

Today's Declaration Challenge: I challenge you today to put God and kingdom first in your endeavors. Kingdom minded persons are always seeking to make God look good and lead others to His presence. They don't do anything for selfish gain, but that God might be glorified. Change your mind to teach others about a new way of thinking. Surround yourself with persons that think higher than where they are. Connect and look for people that are moving forward and not backwards. You don't have time for negativity in your life. Make your choice that today **"I am kingdom-minded."**

Notes

_____

_____

_____

_____

_____

_____

_____

Day 33

"I AM PLANTED"

"He shall be like a tree planted by the rivers of water, that brings forth its fruit in its season, whose leaf also shall not wither; and whatever he does shall prosper."

-Psalm 1:3

Growing on our property, there used to be an apple tree as you entered the driveway. It was a big tree with branches that went over the driveway and was rather tall. It would yield apples in the spring and summer seasons much our fulfillment and that of our horses also. It would become a staple there. It would also become a residence for hornets and bees that would create great big dwellings on branches.

I remember riding a horse and having to brace myself as it ran straight into a branch and nicked my back sequentially. It was a grand tree. Eventually for whatever reason, it was cut down and uprooted years later. One thing that stood out to me was that no matter what season we found ourselves in, at the appropriate time that apple tree would fulfill its purpose and that was to produce apples in its proper time. It was rooted and planted, and it was on a mission.

My friends, no matter what you go through today and what you're facing, you have a responsibility to ensure that you're planted and rooted to fulfill your purpose. In the text for today we see a psalm speaking the pathways of the righteous and those that are ungodly. Though we don't know who exactly wrote Psalm 1, the words hold much weight. It reads at verse 3 "He shall be like a tree, planted by the rivers of water, that brings forth its fruit in its season, whose leaf shall not wither and whatever he does shall prosper."

To be planted, one must take not that you're not easily swayed or altered. When you're planted in God and in His righteousness, he will make you productive. As you labor at your respective place of employment and study in schools of thought or rest in days of retirement, you should desire to remain productive. You should remain relevant. At the end of the day, if you've been planted but have nothing to show for it, you become of no avail. You fruit is of no good.

I also enjoy that verse because it says, "whose leaf also shall not wither." My goodness that's good news. That even as you're going from here to there, God can bless every part of you to be sustained when you're planted in Him. Does that mean that you won't have sick or down moments? No, it does not, but it does mean that He will uphold you even through your dry seasons and your storms.

Where are you planted today? For the place that God has you established, can those around you see your efforts and labor? I'm even more encouraged by the latter part of that verse that says, "and whatever he does shall prosper." When you desire to live for God today and let your roots be planted in Him, he adds prosperity to your efforts. What a blessing to know that God will always take care of His children. That's His desire for you and me today when we plant our feet in Him.

Today's Declaration Challenge: My challenge for you today is to get planted in God and His will for your life. What area of your life are you not as planted and settled as you should be? Once you know and can identify it enough to articulate it or speak on it, seek wisdom from those skilled in that area. If your finances are planted only on payday but soon uprooted on the same day, maybe you need a new foundation. I dare you to seek after a prosperous life that everything you touch lasts. I pray that God would even plant your family and friends in the areas that they've always longed for. Today let God ground you and declare **"I am planted."**

Notes

_____

_____

_____

_____

_____

_____

Day 34

"I AM BETTER"

"But, beloved, we are confident of better things concerning you, yes
things that accompany salvation, though we speak in this manner.
For God is not unjust to forget your work and labor of love which
you have shown toward His name, in that you have ministered to the
saints and do minister."

-Hebrews 6:9-10

My prayer for you today is that the "spirit of better" shall be your portion today and always. There will be so many things that will press against you throughout the order of life and even this day that will try to make you bitter. We cast that spirit out in Jesus' name.

I speak "better" over you today. For Christ did not come into this world, live a sinless life, heal the sick, bring sight to the blind, die on a cross, rise from the dead for us to stay in a place of bitterness. We've already discussed about how Jesus desires to give us "abundant life." Jesus did all that He did for our redemption, our salvation and for our restoration. If we deny His sacrifice, then we defeat ourselves and limit the scope of our potential.

The writer of this text to the Hebrews speaks on this better life through Christ Jesus. In Hebrews 6:9 it states, "But beloved, we are confident of better things concerning you, yes things that accompany salvation though we speak in this manner." The writer lets the believers know that your life with Christ reflects a greater purpose and power than life without Him. He encourages them to let their progress be known. Show and tell of what God has done for you.

You will face giants today while on your journey. You may be right amid remarkable success and accomplishment on the flip side. Regardless of what season you're in, let your progress be shown. By giving out the best of you, you give no room for the enemy to bring out the worst of you.

I speak better over of you. Let better be your portion. How does one live in a state of better you may ask? You do so by relying on the Lord. Psalm 118:8 reads that, "It is better to trust in the Lord than to put confidence in man." Can you say that your life is better since the Lord came into it? Through all that you've seen, heard, witnessed and felt are you confident in declaring better for yourself? Circumstances of life may try to get the best of you but keep living. There's nothing more motivating than a back that's turned on you. There's nothing more uplifting than succeeding around someone that tried to hold you down.

Today's Declaration Challenge: I challenge you to see after your best life. It is possible to face the worst and still win at your best. No matter how you feel, I challenge you to dress up, liven up and speak yourself to a better state. The past is gone. Don't choose to live there anymore. Beloved, ***better*** looks good on you. I speak better to your finances, your faith, family and your mind. Let your voice be heard and declare **"I am better."**

Notes

_____

_____

_____

_____

_____

_____

_____

Day 35

"I AM TESTED"

"For you, O God, have tested us; You have refined us as silver is refined."

-Psalm 66:10

Daily you and I are tested in one way or another. We can't escape it. We're tested while driving and some speed-demon wizzes past us and barely misses our vehicle. We're tested emotionally when we're trying to live a positive and loving life and yet someone who is incapable of doing the same due to their own insecurities, hurts you again. We're tested financially as bills seem to find you quicker than your payroll does, and you must make smart decisions fast.

I've come to realize that tests and trials have no respect for persons. They can happen to the lofty and the low. Positions of power don't exempt us from testing. Being in the worst of states does not disqualify you and I from facing another hurdle. One thing that has helped me the most in going through tests is the hope that each one has an expiration date and a lesson therein.

The writer of Psalms 66 speaks on God's glory and His great works. It later shifts to show how God works on us. Though we don't know the author some attribute this psalm to David. Whoever it is plainly writes and says, "For You, O God have tested us, you have refined us as silver is refined." That's symbolic and powerful because the writer makes it clear that even though we're being tested that it's for our refinement. The refining process is essentially to make us better. It also removes anything from us that is not like God.

Did you learn anything on the last time that you were tested? Someone who was tested indeed was Abraham in Genesis 22. The first verse of that chapter reads "Now it came to pass after these things that God tested Abraham...." Without full knowledge of God's plans, he was sent to Moriah to sacrifice his son Isaac. When he followed God's voice and prepared to offer his son, divine intervention occurred. Verse 11 and 12 reads "But the Angel of the Lord called to him from heaven and said, "Abraham, Abraham!" So, he said, "Here I am." And He said, "Do not lay your hand on the lad, or do anything to him; for now, I know that you fear God, since you have not withheld your son, your only son, from Me." Now that's a tremendous test of faith, obedience and trust in God.

You may not be facing Abraham's test today, but even your test may troublesome. It may cost you some rest but endure. It may cost you a few friends but endure. If your friends couldn't hang in there during your test, maybe they weren't friends at all but spectators. Your test may cause isolation and separation form places of familiarity. Endure it all for the building of your faith and your own refinement. Job said it best in Job 23:10 saying, "But He knows the way I take; When He has tested me, I shall come forth as gold." *Today's Declaration Challenge*: I challenge you today to accept the testing that you go through today. Say what? Yes, I said accept the testing because it is a process that works to your betterment. If they test you on your job, take a deep breath, square your shoulders, clear your mind and persevere. It prunes your character and it makes you better. Without the test there will be no testimony. Without the testimony, you may not be able to fully witness to others about God's grace and power in your life. Be challenged to build your faith. Even though you can't see it while you're in it, let the test run its course and come out with the evidence that you survived. Declare today **"I am tested"** but I have a testimony.

Notes

_____

_____

_____

_____

_____

_____

_____

Day 36

"I AM AMBITIOUS"

"Then she made a vow and said O Lord of hosts, if You will indeed look on the affliction of Your maidservant and remember me and not forget Your maidservant but will give Your maidservant a male child then I will give him to the Lord all the days of his life and no razor shall come upon his head."

-1 Samuel 1:11

What are your ambitions today? Are you making smart money moves towards that long term dream you've had? Are your ambitions of going back to school becoming more prevalent? Maybe your ambitious towards starting a family or even maintaining the current family unit that you have. Whatever your ambitions are, they must always carefully be considered.

Being ambitious or having a desire to achieve a goal is not a dreadful thing. It's a desirable trait to have. The only ambitions that are not the best are the ones that lead to the detriment of another. That in turn becomes thoughts of evil and no one should desire such.

We see ambition on display biblically in the life of Hannah in the Old Testament. She was one of two wives to Elkanah. The other wife had children with Elkanah, but Hannah did not. It was truly her desire and ambition to be a mother. She wept for a child and worshipped God year after year appealing to Him for one to no avail. In her vow to God at the tabernacle, her ambition is heard when she said in 1 Samuel 1:11, "O Lord of hosts, if You will indeed look on the affliction of Your maidservant and remember me, and not forget Your maidservant, but will give Your maidservant a male child, then I will give him to the Lord all the days of his life and no razor shall come upon his head."

What a vow!! She made her request and desire known and even made a vow to give the child back to God upon his arrival. That's ambition indeed. To ask for a thing and then vow to give it back to the giver upon getting it. Do you have that kind of ambition to see things manifest in your reality? Is your ambition all about you or is it towards another? Do you desire to see others blessed? Do you have ambitions towards God's will? Do you have ambitions for a stronger life?

Today's Declaration Challenge: As a believer, I challenge you to be ambitious like Hannah towards the things of God. Let your ambitions be known to Him. When God sees it, He blesses it completely. Be careful of who you share your goals with. Some people may not want to legitimately see you succeed. Be challenged to know that with prayer, effort, determination and an inner drive, God will exceed your imaginations. Declare this day **"I am ambitious."**

Notes

_____

_____

_____

_____

Day 37

"I AM BLESSED BY PROVISION"

"And my God shall supply all your need according to His riches in glory by Christ Jesus."

-Philippians 4:19

If you're like me, at some point in your reality you needed God to grant you more resources to survive. That may be your story today and if it is, that's okay. I've come to realize that God sees the end from the beginning of our stories and He enables us to go through moments of lack as well as seasons of more than enough to know that He's our greatest source when we allow Him to be.

Provision is the act of providing or supplying something for use. It is the very thing needed to meet a need, for a certain people in a moment. I'll never forget a moment in my life where I was in-between work due to a layoff and I was seeking direction. In that time of seeking the next move I was fortunate enough to receive a severance from my previous employer. That provision was indeed sufficient for where I was and to help me towards where I was going.

I'm sure like me, you can recall times where God stepped in and allowed someone to 'pay it forward' on your behalf and bless you in the middle of situation that you weren't expecting. Their provision and assistance were blessed assurance that God was looking out for you where you were. The Apostle Paul had that same assurance at the time of the scripture before us today. Scholars would note that he was in prison upon writing it. He tells the church in Philippi "And my God shall supply all your need according to His riches in glory by Christ Jesus" (Philippians 4:19). God will take care of His own.

Paul is locked up, but he has full hope and confidence that God will look after the needs of the local church and bless the cause of Christ. He gives them consolation that there is no mountain too high that God can't help you overcome. Do you have that kind of hope?

When we take care of God's business, He then takes care of our business. When we acknowledge Him, He then acknowledges us. The Prophet Malachi records in Malachi 3:10 that we are to "Bring all the tithes into the storehouse, that there may be food in My house, and try Me now in this, says the Lord of hosts, If I will not open for you the windows of heaven and pour out for you such blessing that there will not be room enough to receive it." Provision at its best will be more than you dreamed of. I pray that over you today.

Today's Declaration Challenge: Be challenged today that God is providing for you. You may not see it but it's working for your good. Where there is a vision, God always grants provision. I challenge you to even be humble enough to accept the provision of God. God may use whomever He desires to meet your need. It may be a friend, or even an enemy but whoever they are, don't allow false pride to cause you to miss your blessing. Put yourself in the right posture to receive it and declare **"I am blessed by provision."**

Notes

Day 38

"I AM BLESSED BY MY BLOODLINE"

"And behold, the Lord stood above it and said: I am the Lord God of Abraham your father and the God of Isaac; the land on which you lie I will give to you and your descendants."

-Genesis 28:13

You are as great as you are from your bloodline or the connections that you have. It is undeniable that you are a collaboration of maternal and paternal family members that have gone on before you. Whether you realize it or not or even try to hide from it, your character echoes those gone before you. That's why you can do some things or say some things and pause and then say, "I sound just like my mother or my father."

Personal moment: I'll never forget one time I was riding a little beyond the speed limit on a road near my home. Sequentially, some blue lights shined behind me. You know who it was. The officer walks up to my car and asked me where I was going and if he could see my license and registration. I handed it over to him. After a few moments, he returns to the car and says, "Are you related to the Deans that live not far from here?" I replied "Yes." He then hands my license and paperwork and says "Sir, I would write you a ticket for going a little over the speed limit but I'm not going to do it because I know who your dad is. Have a wonderful day and drive safe." The punishment I should have received, I didn't because who I

119

was connected to. To God be the glory.

In the scripture reference for today, we see the Lord God speaking to Jacob in the form of a dream about his lineage. He tells him in Genesis 28:13, "And behold the Lord stood above it and said, "I am the Lord God of Abraham your father and the God of Isaac; the land on which you lie I will give to you and your descendants." God tells Jacob that He had been the God of his father Isaac and his grandfather Abraham. He lets him know that generationally, He blessed and kept them and that He would do the same for Jacob and even His descendants. That's a blessing that we all should desire. The kind that flows from not only our parents to us but also to our children's children.

As you live today, I speak blessings over you and your generations. The kind that supersedes right now. The kind that causes you to always win. What God did for Jacob is a testament to what He promised Abraham in Genesis 12:2 when He told him, "I will make you a great nation; I will bless you and make your name great; And you shall be a blessing." Every generation should desire for their children or those that come after them to go farther and be greater than they could.

You are great because of your bloodline. Whether they all made the best decisions or not, you can be better than they were. You have the blessing of a favored bloodline. You have the power to shape your reality and your future.

Today's Declaration Challenge: My prayer for you is that every generation in your life experiences the covenant of God. I hope that as God did it for Abraham, Isaac and Jacob that He would do the same for you. I pray that even if there is a rift in your ranks that it will be smoothed out. I challenge you to know your worth. Know your power. Know your value. Know the weight that you carry. In knowing this, you walk in the favor of God. You then also live in the grace of God. Make your declaration that **"I am blessed by my bloodline."**

Notes

_____

_____

_____

_____

_____

_____

_____

Day 39

"I AM CONFIDENT"

"I can do all things through Christ who strengthens me."

-Philippians 4:13

To do anything successfully, you will need confidence. Confidence will enable you to do things that you otherwise would not normally do. In all my days, I would have never imagined singing as much as I have in life. Though I have always had a love for it, I never jumped to just quickly sing in every setting. However, when asked to do it, I tried to always oblige musical requests.

Confidence will cause you to speak up for what's right no matter what the cost. It will put you around persons you otherwise may not communicate with or even associate with. Confidence will allow you to step out and pursue that business venture that you've only pondered in your mind. It will propel you to unfamiliar places and opportunities.

Almost every person in the Bible had to have confidence, trust and reliance on God, to accomplish the task that was set before them. Paul writes one of the most recitable scriptures ever in today's focus text. It reads "I can do all things through Christ who strengthens me" (Philippians 4:13). It is believed that he pens these words to unify a church that was divided amongst their ranks.

Paul takes personal inventory over his life. He's thankful for those within the church that availed themselves to helping him in the

122

Lord's service. He recalls being with enough and being without. In distinguishing between the two, he assures the church that if he has Christ nothing can be withheld from him. He finds strength in Christ. You too should desire that kind of assurance.

Do you have such fortitude? Maybe you're up against deadlines and quotas and you don't how you're going to finish? You may need confidence to confront a divisive person that has done all the kind to hinder you and others from moving forward. Your ability to dismiss critics and crush even your own fears, will increase your confidence. Even though Paul was not in the best position, he foresaw himself going beyond that moment. Confidence should work for you in that same manner. See yourself beyond where you are right now.

I pray that the spirit of confidence will be your portion today. As you determine, what life's next move will be, be confident with your decision. Stick to your intuition. Pray that the Holy Spirit would comfort you and enable your confidence to flourish.

Today's Declaration Challenge: My prayer and challenge for you today is that you don't limit yourself. Don't negate your own power and strengths. You did not go through what you've been through to become stagnant and timid. Use what you have. I also challenge you to have confidence not only in yourself but in someone else. Paul had confidence for others as well as he states in 2 Corinthians 7:16, "Therefore I rejoice that I have confidence in you in everything." Be strong enough to support and push another to their place of confidence. You may be just the boost of encouragement they need. Make your declaration today, **"I am confident."**

Notes

_____

_____

_____

_____

_____

_____

_____

Day 40

"I AM BOLD"

"In the day when I cried out, You answered me, And made me bold with strength in my soul."

-Psalm 138:3

Do you consider yourself to be bold? Do you have a boldness about you that is undeniable? *Merriam-Webster Dictionary* records the definition of bold as showing or requiring a fearless spirit. Being bold allows you to not allow what you see to hinder what you believe.

Everyone should desire to be bold in this life. Boldness is seen in parents, who don't mind speaking up in defense of their child, whether they know if they're right or wrong. Boldness is seen in the business world where employees take on projects that are bigger than them, with the confidence to complete them. Boldness is shown when you can go directly to the source of trouble or pain, confront it to make it better.

The scripture reference for this declaration comes from David. He makes it known in Psalm 138:3 saying, "In the day when I cried out, You answered me, And made me bold with strength in my soul." He states that God made him bold with strength even in his soul. Beloved, I pray that God will overshadow you with a boldness that you know not of. David went from crying to boldness. I pray that over you today. The old way of wallowing in your sorrow shall be no more. Boldness belongs to you.

I've come to believe and espouse that the thing that keeps me from living boldly, is the opinions or thoughts of others. Thinking or being bound by the thoughts of others will have you stuck in a place of doing nothing. You must be delivered today from what people will say, and know what you will say and do. Be bold to let your 'Yes' be Yes and your 'No' be No as Matthew 5:37 reads.

I submit to you today that your blessings are tied to your boldness. The writer of Hebrews 4:16 penned, "Let us therefore come boldly to the throne of grace, that we may obtain mercy and find grace to help in the time of need." There's blessings awaiting you today out of your boldness. Mercy and grace are assigned to you, when you can go to God with an attitude of fearlessness and boldness. I don't know about you, but I don't want my timid way to cause me to miss my blessing.

Can you readily identify areas of life today that you need boldness? The magnitude of your boldness can set the captive free. When you go after God, your dreams and desires, with boldness, it opens the door to your next place.

Today's Declaration Challenge: I challenge you to simply be bold. There are some things that are bound right now that only your boldness will unloose. Be bold enough to ask God for the things you need to be better. Be challenged to know your own worth. Let your boldness be evident. Let it send your enemies to flee from you. Today declare **"I am bold."**

Notes

_____

_____

_____

_____

_____

_____

_____

Day 41

"I AM ON ASSIGNMENT"

"Now the word of the Lord came to Jonah the son of Armittai, saying, Arise, go to Nineveh, that great city, and cry out against it; for their wickedness has come up before Me."

-Jonah 1:1-2

Today, you have a unique opportunity to do things you may not have done before on a day that you have never seen. For each thing that God has allowed you to do and will do, your perspective concerning it makes the difference. It becomes not a to-do list but rather assignments.

As you may journey to school, work or the sofa in retirement, you have assignments that you must complete. For many, the things that they're assigned to, are always bigger than them. Many assignments are lengthy at times and last longer than even you may desire. There is a joy that comes in remaining close to and on task in life. Someone may quickly witness, that they may not have understood why they were chosen to do certain things in life, but they were so glad that they did in the end.

What happens when we don't stay on assignment? Who better to tell us today than the Prophet Jonah? Jonah was given directions to preach against the city of Nineveh. Preaching was his calling. He was supposed to point the persons he preached to a place of repentance. Jonah had other plans or was defiant because in Jonah

1:3 reads, "But Jonah arose to flee to Tarshish from the presence of the Lord." Now I don't know what Jonah's deal was or what he may have been going through, but seemingly he was out of his mind. He intentionally went the opposite way. I know you can't see this because you're reading this but imagine going west and God needed for you to go east. He went left, when God wanted him to go right!

God sent a storm to go against the ship Jonah was on. The men threw him overboard when they discovered that he was the cause of the storm and then Jonah was swallowed up by a great fish. All of this happened due to his disobedience. When you stay on your assignment, you avoid unnecessary trouble. Jonah eventually was spit out by the fish and told again to go to Nineveh. He goes and preaches, and something happens. Jonah 3:5 says, "So the people of Nineveh believed God, proclaimed a fast, and put on sackcloth, from the greatest to the least of them." What a change and what an assignment!

My friend, understand and know that the thing God has called you to and assigned to you has nothing to do with you. Say what? Yes, your assignment is bigger than your feelings. There are lives attached to it. There's repentance and salvation connected to you doing what God has assigned you to. The places that God has assigned you to a greater than what you see but, in your obedience,, He always rewards your efforts.

Today's Declaration Challenge: You can't listen to naysayers on your assignment. Stay on task. Stay on track. I challenge you to put your agenda to the side for the assignment of God. It may be different. It may stretch you and pull you beyond your level of comfort, but it is ordained for you. Embrace your God given assignment. It may lead you to strangers. It may lead you to do uncommon things. It may cause you to scratch your head but it's for your good. As you go about this day, declare **"I am on assignment."**

Notes

_____

_____

_____

_____

_____

_____

_____

Day 42

"I WAS LOST BUT NOW I AM FOUND"

"Or what woman, having ten silver coins, if she loses one coin, does not light a lamp, sweep the house and search carefully until she finds it? And when she has found it, she calls her friends and neighbors together, saying, 'Rejoice with me, for I have found the piece which I lost!' Likewise, I say to you, there is joy in the presence of the angels of God over one sinner who repents."

-Luke 15:8-10

Every one of us can recall a time that we were lost. It matters not if you were lost in a department store, in the wrong neighborhood or in a world of sin, lost is lost. We all have been there. It doesn't matter how long you've been lost. You're only desire ultimately is to not be lost ever again.

I'll never forget one time when I was a child, that I became separated from my parents in a department store. I don't know what I was doing. I clearly wasn't paying attention to my surroundings and after a few moments of not seeing my family, panic began to set in. I went all over trying to find them. I didn't want to be on the milk carton as a missing kid.

I remember going to a store clerk and having them call for my parents on the loudspeaker and they eventually found me. That never happened again during my childhood. The joy I had at being found was beyond this world.

The same joy is found in the scriptures for today. Jesus uses the parables of the lost in Luke 15 in a unique manner. He talks about the lost sheep, the lost son and the lost coin. He speaks of this woman who searches for her lost coin in her home. Luke 15:9 reads, "And when she has found it, she calls her friends and neighbors together saying, 'Rejoice with me, for I have found the piece which I lost!' Likewise I say to you, there is joy in the presence of the angels of God over one sinner who repents." That's a blessing by itself.

You may be lost today in a minor way. You may feel lost in this world. You may feel that you lack purpose or power to live your best life. It is possible to be in a crowded room and still feel lost. You may desire to be found and saved from the affairs of this life. Let me encourage you today that God is awaiting your return. He is looking for you and what you have to offer. God also desires for you to be found and to inwardly find yourself.

You will at some point run across someone who is lost and not know it. It happens. Instead of looking down on their predicament, approach them where they are in peace. Speak life to them. Talk them through their pain and you'll win a soul. The peace that they're looking for, you may have. The joy they desire, may be in your possession. Point them towards a new-found life in God alone. Understand this, you can be lost in the house. You can be where you need to be and still not be fully together.

Today's Declaration Challenge: Be found today in peace. Be found in joy. I challenge you to seek after being found in a well-state. God desires for you to be complete and whole. I also challenge you to help others who are lost to find their way. Understand and know that their way may not be yours. Their timing may not be yours. Your understanding of where a lost person is, will better help you in serving them until their found. Today make a declaration that **"I was lost but now I am found."**

Notes

_____

_____

_____

_____

_____

_____

_____

Day 43

"I AM INSPIRED"

"All Scripture is given by inspiration of God, and is profitable for doctrine, for reproof, for correction, for instruction in righteousness."

-2 Timothy 3:16

Prayerfully this devotional has uplifted and inspired you in your daily walk with God. As a supplement to your own daily Bible reading, my prayer is that it has inspired you in some way to use your words to shape your reality. Inspiration is solely the purpose of this work.

With that said, what inspires you? What motivates you? For me personally, the word of God inspires me daily to continue this fight of life. Music also inspires me as I hear an intro of a song, to the vamp and its ending. I'm inspired by family and friends, who have a tenacity to not let what they experience stop them from what they believe and living from day to day. These things inspire me.

The Apostle Paul, who was put into ministry after being a persecutor of Christians, was inspired by Christ to live for Him. So inspired and taken was he, that he spent the rest of his life establishing churches, preaching and building them up to remain with God. At the time of this text in 2 Timothy 3:16, he tells his mentee Timothy, "All Scripture is given by inspiration of God, and is profitable for doctrine, for reproof, for correction, for instruction in righteousness." He lets him know that God inspired the words that you read as biblical scriptures. By His inspiration, the words of life are read and preached from, for our training and development.

I pose the question to you again, what inspires you? You may be at a place where you're inspired by seeing others well and taken care of. You may be inspired by working on that craft that was your first love. Inspiration may come to you through the rhythms of music to hear more. However it comes, let what inspires you to guide your actions today.

Ultimately, God was and is the source that enabled you to do what you do. Just like He did it for the writers and disciples of old to pen biblical truth, He's inspiring you to get things done. What do you need to finish that you left undone? Let your inspiration continue to work for you. Just as God's word is a "lamp unto our feet and a light unto our path" (Psalm 118:105), your inspiration will last on your behalf for a long time.

Today's Declaration Challenge: Be inspired to believe again for the impossible. Be inspired to run this race of life with endurance. Your inspiration is not to be wasted. No one is inspired to be stagnant and lazy. Put your calling to use. Don't let your aspirations die with you. Someone is waiting on you to do what you've been called to. I challenge you to be inspired to live your best life today. Declare **"I am inspired."**

Notes

Day 44

"I AM LOOKING UP"

"I will lift up my eyes to the hills- From whence comes my help? My help comes from the Lord, who made heaven and earth."

-Psalm 121:1

What are you looking at? That's not only a question that we all have heard at some point in our lives, but one that we should seriously consider. We should consider it because whatever thing or direction that we find ourselves focusing on will be the trajectory that our lives will go. For example, if I'm always looking downward at some point I'm not going to focus on what's ahead of me and either crash into something or go in the wrong way.

The writer of this psalm, though anonymous in identity, gave directions on where our focus should be as believers. Psalm 121:1 reads, "I will lift up my eyes to the hills- From whence comes my help? My help comes from the Lord." Ironically, in Jewish custom, Jews returned to Jerusalem for several feasts throughout the year. Jerusalem sat on an elevated hill. As the people entered higher into the city, they would sing "songs of ascents."

I appreciate the writer of this psalm, because they point us all in the way that we should be looking. Upward should always be our desire. Our help is not found in the hills. It is the act of looking up where the hills are and beyond them. Our help comes from God.

Are you looking up or are you bound to a downward

direction? It's hard to seek help on the level that you're on. Why is that? We can aide each other in some ways but no help can supersede the help of God.

The psalmist would go on to describe how God never sleeps nor slumbers nor will He let your foot be moved (Psalm 121:3-4). That's great news today. No matter how life tries to press you down, keep looking up. You may be facing immense debt and don't know how you're going to overcome it, but keep looking up. Your career may be changing and challenging you to where you don't know how you'll endure it, but keep looking up. Things may be prospering for you to pursue a degree or finally buy the house of your dreams but keep looking up. You're not looking at the clouds but rather looking upward to God, to keep you humble and regarding Him as the keeper of your soul.

Today's Declaration Challenge: Keep your head to the sky. Things will get hard. You will desire to quit. You will want to throw in the towel. You will not know it all and that's fine. You're not God. If He's in control, and you "look unto Jesus as the author and finisher of your faith" (Hebrews 12:2), you cannot go wrong. By seeking Him and His will, He then settles you, If you keep your eyes on Him, you won't be swayed by this world. Let your declaration be known today that **"I am looking up."**

Notes

_____

_____

Day 45

"I AM TRUSTING GOD"

"Trust in the Lord with all your heart, And lean not on your own understanding; In all your ways acknowledge Him, And He shall direct your paths."
-Proverbs 3:5-6

My friends, if you don't do anything else in this life, you should always trust in God. As a matter of fact, if you can't trust in anyone else in this world, you can always trust in God. The idea of trusting in anything is hard because we live in a time of much skepticism and distrust among many in this world. Skepticism because many people have a challenging time believing the outer shell of anyone else to be genuine. Distrust is common because many people have trusted in others and have had that trust broken in the process.

Those that are wise, tend to know that trust should not be taken lightly and just given to any and everybody. King Solomon wrote to his sons on this very thing. He wanted to ensure that they were wise in their judgements and decisions. He tells them in Proverbs 3:5, "Trust in the lord with all your heart, And lean not on your own understanding; In all your ways acknowledge Him, And He shall direct your paths." Those are indeed words to live by. I don't know what you may dealing with, but I know that I need God to direct my paths. In trusting Him, we find that he makes crooked places straight. He takes over when we don't rely on our own understanding or way of doing things.

Are you trusting in God? For that mother that is trying to instruct your children in the way that they should go, put your trust in God. To that father that desires to posture yourself in a way to exemplify the strong counsel to your child, trust in God. For that ministry leader and worker that is frustrated and tired of dealing with the ways of unreliable persons, turn your focus and trust back to God.

Solomon's father, David understood the importance of walking and trusting in God. He stated in Psalm 37:3, "Trust in the Lord, and do good; Dwell in the land. And feed on His faithfulness." When your trust is in God, you don't have to waste your time concerned with things that are futile. You can find rest in Him and His faithfulness to know that He's working things out for you in the end. God won't let you be ashamed either when you trust Him. Psalm 25:2 reads, "O my God, I trust in You; Let me not be ashamed; Let not my enemies triumph over me." It does us good to keep our trust in God.

Is your trust in things? Honestly speaking there are many people who have trust but it's in the wrong things. They trust in their jobs, their possessions, their vehicles and other things that are temporary. That seems to be a very self-defeating way to live. I say that because if I place my trust in my money, I could have it today and lose it tomorrow. If I trust in the car I drive, it may not be reliable in my time of need. Psalm 20:7 reads, "Some trust in chariots, and some in

horses; But we will remember the name of the Lord our God."
Beloved, it's better to trust in the Lord above anything else.

Today's Declaration Challenge: Where does your trust lie? Is it in people? Now don't get me wrong, I'm not telling you to not have persons in life that you can put your trust in. You do need persons in life that you can trust. I am telling you that at the end of the day, God needs your trust to the utmost. I challenge you to trust God enough to tell God about what you're up against before you tell social media. I challenge you to guard your heart. Be wise in your decisions. If you have trust issues, let God heal your heart and give you discernment before giving out your trust again. Today declare **"I am trusting God."**

Notes

_____

_____

_____

_____

_____

_____

Day 46

"I AM TAKEN CARE OF"

"Casting all your care upon Him, for He cares for you."

-1 Peter 5:7

God is taking care of you. Never forget that. Take comfort in that very fact. No matter where you go in life and for every phase of your life, be fully aware that the Lord has been with you. He is our strength and our guide through the channels of time. From your early childhood days, when you didn't have a care in the world. To your adolescent years, when you began to find your independence. To your young adult life, where you went where you wanted to go and did what you wanted to do. Even through your middle years, where you became more settled and established, He was there. His care has and will be, present for you when you need it most.

My friends, in knowing that God has cared for you throughout your days, may I ask you, why is it that we get bogged down in worry and doubt? Why do we stress ourselves out trying to carry everything on our shoulders? Why do we lose sleep caring about things or people that have shown you and I that they don't care for us? Not only is that silly but it can make us sick trying to spend all our spirits trying to care for and carry everything. If you're doing this, stop it right now.

In the scripture reference for today, Peter the Apostle and disciple of Christ, writes to the early believers about this subject. He tells them in 1 Peter 5:7, "casting all your care upon Him, for He cares for you." He gives them the assurance to be mindful of where you cast your cares. It must be stated that there are persons that are incapable of carrying the weight of your cares. There are people that suffer with the inability of receiving your concerns in love. At word of your problems, they will quickly be hired as tv reporters and spread your business faster than you could turn around. Peter makes it clear by saying that God cares for us.

Do you have that testimony today? Can you identify ways that He cares for you? When others leave you, God will be there. David speaks on the care of the Lord in Psalms 27:10 saying, "When my father and my mother forsake me, Then the Lord will take care of me." That's good news today.

If at any moment today, you find yourself questioning if anyone cares for you, dismiss that thought. God will be there with you when everyone else is gone. His presence will overshadow you with peace and comfort. When circumstances come and try to depress you and oppress you from moving forward, find hope in the shepherd. The thing about a shepherd is that they care for their sheep. Jesus says in John 10:11, "I am the good shepherd. The good shepherd gives His life for His sheep." To give your life for another is the ultimate sign of care.

Today's Declaration Challenge: Examine your connections today. If you're connected to anyone that does not genuinely and godly care for you, you're headed down a damaging road. One of the most giving things we can do is care for the needs of others. I dare to accept the care of the Lord. Release any concerns off you that are holding you back from being at your best. Give those cares to God. It makes no sense to carry heavy loads that don't belong to you. Let God's care reside with you today. If you're undergoing stress and tragedy, you don't have to go at it alone. He will supply your needs and give you more than enough. His care is endless. Let God in and declare **"I am taken care of."**

Notes

_____

_____

_____

_____

_____

_____

_____

Day 47

"I AM COMMISSIONED"

"Go therefore and make disciples of all the nations, baptizing them in the name of the Father and of the Son and of the Holy Spirit, teaching them to observe all things that I have commanded you; and lo I am with you always, even to the end of the age." Amen.
-Matthew 28:19-20

God has commissioned you to do mighty things. He has placed life in you today, not for a show or for your selfish ambition. He gave you new life to tell others about His goodness. God has mapped out the course of our days and even detailed those that we would encounter.

It is an awesome thing to consider. When we really look over the course of our lives, we will see that there were persons that we strategically met along the way that were in desperate situations. In their desperation, God allowed you to be a light in a dark place. He allowed your voice to witness of a Savior that redeemed you. My friends, in those moments you were living out the Great Commission.

As believers, when we gather together in worship and while we're out in the fields of life, we should always desire to carry out this commission. It is the directives for an effective disciple. We see these words so greatly spoken by Jesus the Christ, as He appeared to His disciples. He tells them in Matthew 28: 19-20a, "Go therefore and make disciples of all the nations, baptizing them in the name of the Father and of the Son and of the Holy Spirit, teaching them to observe all things that I have commanded you;" Jesus gives instructions that we all can glean from and it is that we are disciples anywhere we are. We are called to go out and look for disciples as well as teach those who we find about His grace and power. By baptism in His name, we seal them under the Lord's care.

You may say to yourself, "I'm not a preacher or minister. I don't have to disciple others to Christ." Well, that may be true as far as your title or position, but you don't have to be a minister or great orator to lead others to a life of discipleship. Being a disciple is not about a position, but it is about being in the right posture at the right time to inspire others about God's grace and ultimate sacrifice. It's one of the best things you can ever do for a person.

Today, you may encounter someone that is in a troublesome place. As you speak to them, you as a believer, have a responsibility to give them the words of life. You don't have to shout at them or raise your voice, but you can simply give them hope and love as Christ has given it to you. Jeremiah 31:3 reads, "Therefore even with lovingkindness I have drawn you." God spoke such to the Prophet Jeremiah to the Israelites, to display His unending love for His chosen people. Just as God loved Israel and commissioned His prophets to give them correction, guidance and love, He loves you too.

Today's Declaration Challenge: Walk in your God-given,

commissioned power. You are the voice that God will use in this hour. You should have a desire to see others come to the saving power of God. Do you need to be pushy? No, but you can be compassionate. I challenge you to seek after moments to share the gospel. Share the good news. Share about what God has done for you. Today let someone know **"I am commissioned"** to share the good news with you.

Notes

_____

_____

_____

_____

_____

_____

_____

Day 48

"I AM SUPPORTIVE"

"Rejoice with those who rejoice, and weep with those who weep. Be of the same mind toward one another. Do not set your mind on high things, but associate with the humble. Do not be wise in your own opinion."

-Romans 12:15-16

It matters not if you're independent and well established, you need the support of others. I will forever be thankful for persons that have supported me in my life like my parents, who support my brothers and I consistently. Persons such as my Aunt Ruth, that typically goes wherever I am preaching, rain, sleet or snow. She's been a help. Not only should we be thankful for persons that support us, but we should also support others as they reach their goals.

People don't have to be nice to you and when they are, you should show your appreciation towards them. Support is two-fold. Paul speaks on being there for others in Romans 12:15-16 saying, "Rejoice with those who rejoice, and weep with those who weep. Be of the same mind toward one another. Do not set your mind on high things, but associate with the humble. Do not be wise in your own opinion." He gives wise counsel that we should be there for each other. Life will get hard, and when it does, you need to have persons in your life that will settle you and comfort you. In the same way, there will be joys and great moments in your life. You will also need persons to celebrate with as they would do the same for you.

Essentially, support should be mutual. If you find yourself today rendering support to someone for prolonged periods of time and it's not reciprocal, maybe that's not support but dependency. You will wear yourself out if you're pulling someone along all the time. It's taxing on you. Luke writes in Acts 20:35, "I have shown you in every way, by laboring like this, that you must support the weak. And remember the words of the Lord Jesus, that He said, "It is more blessed to give than to receive." Jesus even desires for us to live a life where we give and show support to others. The key to that is we're more blessed when we give not expecting to receive anything, but we do it out of the kindness of our hearts.

How is your support system? Are you supportive of your friends and family? If you are not, how can you be? Are you able to incorporate more time for your loved ones? You will find that your life will be more blessed when you are there for others and they're present for you also. One thing we cannot get back is time. You may be able to earn more money, but you can't earn opportunities to be supportive in life. When you bear another's burdens, they in time will do the same for you.

Today's Declaration Challenge: Support those around you, as you can. Be a listening ear for someone in their weakness. Shorten an appointment to be with your family. Do something you may not be interested in, even though it makes your friends happy. Share your burdens with someone you trust. Take the trip with your crew. It may cost you some free time, but it will build your bond. Stretch yourself to be a help to others. Check on your strong friend. They should not have to check on you all the time. Let mutuality be your portion. Press yourself today to be firmly say **"I am supportive."**

Notes

_____

_____

_____

_____

_____

_____

_____

Day 49

"I AM ON MY WAY"

"Because narrow is the gate and difficult is the way which leads to life, and there are few who find it."
-Matthew 7:14

You are going somewhere in life. You are meant and destined to go great distances. No one should always remain where they started. Even more so, you should never remain where others left you. People will try their best to drop you like a bad habit by their inability to see the favor on you. Stay on course.

We all have our certain way that we love to see things done. We all desire to go the way that we have mapped out in our minds. It's natural. Even when you go short distances, we must follow our normal routine way of doing things.

As a person of faith, you may quickly notice that when you give your heart to God, you had to change lanes from your will to His. It is not an easy task to do. The pathway to life is tedious to remain on, as it pertains to a godly direction, but it is possible. Jesus tells His disciples in Matthew 7:13-14, "Enter by the narrow gate; for wide is the gate and broad is the way that leads to destruction, and there are many who go in by it. Because narrow is the gate and difficult is the way which leads to life, and there are few who find it."

Jesus tells them that many people will not choose the better way to go. The way to destruction will be full of unbelief. It will be crowded with those that made up their mind to go that way. On the flip side, there is new life awaiting those that stay on the narrow road. Rather than head down a destructive path, we should daily posture ourselves to go the right way.

Are you on your way on the narrow road? Are you pressing towards the direction that leads to life? We do ourselves a major disservice when we willingly take steps down a destructive path. Are you making strides to heal your family? Are your relationships secure enough to move ahead or are you bound to old issues? Can your colleagues see the direction that you're on?

Your progress should be evident. Your direction in life should be the light of your life. I dare you to choose the way of God. In 2 Samuel 22:31 reads, "As for God, His way is perfect; The word of the Lord is proven; He is a shield to all who trust in Him." David sang those words after the defeat of Goliath. He had seen for himself, the value in staying in the way of God. I encourage you to know that if it seems like you have giants and hurdles in front of you, God has a way for your escape. There is nothing that you will face today that will be so great that God won't see you through.

Let Jesus be your guide. He told His disciples in John 14:6, "Jesus said to him, 'I am the way, the truth, and the life. No one comes to the Father except through Me." He is the light in your direction and He will enable you to stay on the right road.

Today's Declaration Challenge: Which way are you on? Are you determined to take the road less traveled? Can you go without others with you? Stay on the right road. Don't run with the pack. Follow your directions. Be encouraged to not let anything pull out of the way of God's love, peace and favor. Keep Christ with you today. He will humble you and settle your heart. Don't compare your pathway to others? No two courses should ever be the same. Let your faith rise in you in moments of trials. I challenge to you keep your focus and declare **"I am on my way."**

Notes

Day 50

"I AM IN THE RIGHT POSTURE"

"He went a little farther and fell on His face, and prayed, saying, "O My Father, if it is possible, let this cup pass from me, nevertheless, not as I will, but as You will."

-Matthew 26:39

The right posture will do wonders in your circumstances. A posture is the position that a person takes or puts themselves in. It can also be viewed as an attitude or pose. It is the set form that one takes to go from start to finish effectively and productively.

Every singer knows that to properly execute songs and sing thoroughly, they need to be in the right posture. You can't be lazy or slouched down, and push out strong notes. A pilot who flies a plan regularly cannot have the pilot's chair in a reclined position and expect to make it safely where they're going. For anyone that is desirous of a better position in their career, they must understand the importance of readying themselves emotionally, physically and intellectually for where they are trying to go. Ultimately, one cannot expect greater, if they have not postured and prepared themselves for it.

We see Jesus in a different position in the text today. He's in the Garden of Gethsemane, as His betrayal is approaching. He gets distressed thinking of what He was up against and in Matthew 26:39 reads, "He went a little farther and fell on His face, and prayed saying, 'O My Father, if it is possible, let this cup pass from Me; nevertheless, not as I will, but as You will." Though He was facing one of the hardest decisions of His life, the posture He took here is significant. He fell on His face in prayer. He humbled himself before talking to God.

I submit to you today that unless we're able to change our posture in humility, then we can't fully approach God. Daniel understood this. We see that "he knelt down on his knees three times that day, and prayed and gave thanks before his God," (Daniel 6:10). By kneeling, he reverenced the presence of God. David, the psalmist also honored God in a different posture. Psalm 141:2 reads, "Let my prayer be set before You as incense, The lifting up of my hands as the evening sacrifice."

In each person's life, they put themselves in a different posture to pray to God. Whether it was the lifting of hands, putting their face to the ground or getting on their knees in prayer, they changed their position. How's your posture? By faith, we have a mandate and example on how to approach God. Your posture for success, longevity and security must be found in prayer. Your posture prepares you to commune with God. It grants access to Him in a lowly state that prepares you to go higher.

Today's Declaration Challenge: Check your posture today. When things go from right to left, make sure your position is consistent. I challenge you to get in a different stance of doing things. Your choice to get in the right posture, propels you to speak to and hear from God. Many times we take on the posture of our peers. If they complain, we complain. If they get mad, we get mad. If they don't speak life, neither do we. The posture that you take today may not be popular, but it is yours. I'd rather be in the best posture for my life, than not be based on what someone else does. Communicate with God today and declare **"I am in the right posture."**

Notes

_____

_____

_____

_____

_____

_____

_____

Day 51

"I AM A DREAMER"

"Now when they saw him afar off, even before he came near them,
they conspired against him to kill him. Then they said to one another,
"Look this dreamer is coming!"
-Genesis 37:18-19

Are you living your dream? Are you working towards those dreams? Many times, we dream things that seem outlandish or different from our reality. They appear so real and just what we need or other times what we don't need. That's why we can either have nice dreams or nightmares.

I always remember my dreams consisted of me running from someone or racing. They were always wild. Jumping from something or crazy stuff like that. The act of dreaming, though it happens while we're sleeping, it can happen as a vision, daydream or goal while we're awake.

I believe that you should always pursue your dreams in life. There are some endeavors that have been on your heart since your childhood, that you let slip on into the background. You had intentions of going after them and other things happened to cause a setback. Keep pressing on. It's nothing more upsetting than seeing your dream or goal prospering in someone else's hand. In other words, go after your dreams no matter what.

A person that was noted in the Bible as a dreamer, was a

young man named Joseph. Genesis 37:19 speaks of how his brothers saw him, saying, "Then they said to one another, Look this dreamer is coming." They made this statement with malice in their hearts. They did not appreciate his dreams. They knew him as a dreamer, but they did not have an affinity for him or his dreams, because they would seemingly put them in a dimmer light to his bright light. My friend be careful of people who don't celebrate your dream.

There will be people just like Joseph's brothers in your face or even in your ear today, that struggle honoring the dream in you. They are "dream killers." They cannot be happy or even clap for you. They're usually negative whenever you speak about your dream out of fear that it will eclipse them. They fail to understand, that if God gave you a dream, He can do the same for them. They would rather kill your dream or hope, rather than support it. That's a sad way to live. Don't stoop to the level of persons like this in your life.

Work towards your dreams. Sometimes God will give you a dream as a warning of something approaching. The wise men went to Bethlehem to find Baby Jesus after his birth at Herod's request. Upon their arrival, they worshipped Him and gave gifts to Him, but when it was time to go, Matthew 2:12 reads, "Then being divinely warned in a dream that they should not return to Herod, they departed for their own country another way." God will speak to you in a dream. Heed the dreams that God gives you. It will protect you every time. By discerning dreams, you will save yourself and others connected to you.

By running after the dreams and goals that God gives you, you can alter the path of your life. When you are not distracted by doubters of your dreams, you can focus on getting them done. Joseph's dreams were really for his brothers' protection, but they were too ignorant to realize it. They sold him off but after God's favor and elevation rested on him, they needed what he had in the end. Let the dreamer in you arise today.

Today's Declaration Challenge: I challenge you my friends, to not give up on your dreams. You were given them for a reason. If you're already working in your dream, my prayer for you is that you will be sustained to see them through to the end. Put your dreams to action in such a strong way that others know that it belongs to you. Don't be distracted by someone else's inability to recognize your baby (your dream). Lift your voice today and declare **"I am a dreamer."**

Notes

_____

_____

_____

_____

_____

_____

_____

Day 52

"I AM IN DEMAND"

"Let our master now command your servants, who are before you, to seek out a man who is skillful player on the harp. And it shall be that he will play it with his hand when the distressing spirit from God is upon you and you shall be well. So Saul said to his servants, Provide me now a man who can play well, and bring him to me."

-1 Samuel 16:16-17

There is a demand on your life today. You should know it. God has a need of you in His kingdom but be mindful that so does your adversary. The enemy wants your plans to fail though God desires for you to win. What a distinction to understand.

Daily you can feel the pull of your connections to be here or there. As a young person, you may feel the demand to grow up and go to the right schools or pursue the best career. As a parent, there is a demand on your life to shape and mold your child in the best way that they should go. As an entrepreneur, you face demands often, to meet budgets, deadlines and produce something that's lasting for your clientele. As an older adult, you must deal with the demands of remaining active and healthy in an ever-changing world.

I suggest to you today that the demand on your life spiritually, should be foremost in your life today. This kind of demand comes from God alone. It is a demand to use the experiences and lessons of your life for a greater purpose. Such was the case for young David. He grew up as a shepherd boy but also as a great musician. He enjoyed singing and playing instruments before the Lord. He was gifted in the more than one arena and God blessed him for it.

At the time of this text, he was recently anointed as the next king of Israel by the Prophet Samuel. Since David was anointed, Saul's anointing left him. God resisted Saul because he did not listen to Him or heed his direction and was a man of war. This transition of God's anointing is symbolic. God's spirit can leave one and rest on another as He wills it. This caused Saul to be distressed. His advisors sought out help for him thinking that music would soothe him. In 1 Samuel 16:17-18, it reads, "So Saul said to his servants, Provide me now a man who can play well, and bring him to me." Then one of the servants answered and said, 'Look I have seen a son of Jesse the Bethlehemite, who is skillful in playing, a mighty man of valor, a man of war, prudent in speech, and a handsome person; and the Lord is with him." God granted David exposure in this moment like no other.

This is how God works. He will put something in you that others don't have but, yet they need it in their life. He will place a demand for your life so strongly that only you are equipped for, in that moment. You could be experiencing a demand to be in several places at the same time. You may feel pressure to get everything done and done right. I speak life to you, that you're going into a season of overflow in your schedule and your abilities. You are not only called for it but qualified to do mighty things.

Today's Declaration Challenge: My prayer for you is simple. I pray that you are in such a demand that all that you are can handle the favor, appointments, and grace assigned to your life. I challenge you to be so great at the level that you're on right now, that God cannot help but propel you to a new place because you will have outgrown this level. The demand on your life to be exceptional is based on your ability and capacity to believe in you. I challenge you to be your own cheerleader and critic. By doing this, you remain confident and humbled. People need the gifts that you have. This world needs you. Don't negate who you are. Decide to lift your voice **"I am in demand."**

Notes

_____

_____

_____

_____

_____

_____

_____

Day 53

"I AM A VISIONARY"

"Then the Lord answered me and said: Write the vision and make it plain on tablets, that he may run who reads it. For the vision is yet for an appointed time; But at the end it will speak and it will not lie."

-Habakkuk 2:2-3a

What vision do you have for your life? Do you see yourself fulfilling your dreams? Are you optimistic about life or are you pessimistic? The attitude that you take towards your vision ushers it into existence. The moves you make today ensure the accessibility of your vision.

Personally, every year that I live, I try to sit down and write realistic goals for that year. It's something that I do strategically. I try to make goals that I can push towards and that are attainable. By putting them on paper, I also place them where I can easily see them. When I see the vision or goals daily or weekly, I'm more prone to work towards those goals. Many people now create vision boards, which are boards posted with pictures of things that they desire to do.

When God gives you a vision for your life, you must take heed. The Prophet Habakkuk was eager for God to speak to him. He had readied himself for it. God speaks to him in Habakkuk 2:2-3 saying, "Write the vision and make it plain on tablets, that he may run who reads it. For the vision is yet for an appointed time; but at the end it will speak and it will not lie." As the prophet, he had a call on his life to give a word to God's chosen people. He had to look forward to speaking the voice of God.

Visionaries are persons that can glance ahead and predict things happening. They may not know every little detail but they can see enough to know what steps that they need to take. Having a vision is integral to your survival. Proverbs 29:18 reads, "Where there is no vision, the people perish: but he that keeps the law, happy is he (KJV)." If you have a vision before you, you will live proficiently. That's how strong a vision will work for you. It will push you to continue beyond this present moment.

As visionaries, sometimes the visions you have are not for you. We saw that with Habakkuk and Paul. He tells the king in Acts 26:19-20, "Therefore, King Agrippa, I was not disobedient to the heavenly vision, but declared first to those in Damascus and in Jerusalem, and throughout all the region of Judea and then to the Gentiles, that they should repent, turn to God, and do the works befitting repentance." The word that God gives to you may not always be for you but it can call others out from where they are. That's how the vision of God works. It works for the present and even a time that you and I have yet to see.

What vision do you have for your family? What goals do you have for your friends and associates? When was the last time you pressed your way towards a vision that you could not get overnight? The blessing in vision is that it gives you a goal to reach at the end of the day and the road. It gives you something to hope for and press after.

Today's Declaration Challenge: Are you mindful of your vision? Are you thinking of the things that God has given you or are you caught up on someone else's temporary endeavors? Don't get me wrong, it's good to help others vision come to pass. In fact, you should be readily available to assist another's vision if it is in your power to. It's a sign of support, love and care. In doing that, you should never push your vision to a place of desolation to your own detriment when God wants to help you bring it to pass. Your vision may be for someone else's turnaround. It may be for someone else's empowerment but run after it. Keep your eyes open. Keep your faith up. Open your mouth and speak today that **"I am a visionary."**

Notes

_____

_____

_____

_____

_____

_____

_____

Day 54

"I AM A SOLDIER"

"You therefore must endure hardship as a good soldier of Jesus Christ."

-2 Timothy 2:3

Soldiers are those individuals who have made a commitment to give their all to serving the land and country at which they live. I'll never forget growing up and seeing my father serve in the United States Marine Corps. He was dedicated to the cause of being a soldier in the military. He would serve for 22 years and has many vast experiences therein.

For those of us who believe, there is a greater call for us to serve in the army of the Lord. We, who God has called us out of darkness and into his marvelous light, have a responsibility to fight for the Lord as we live. We must take on the garments of war to win souls for God. We must be strong enough to call out the works of the devil so that the lives of others can always be the better.

Paul writes to Timothy, his mentee, at the time of this text. He has done all in his power to train and equip him for ministry and all it entails. He tells Timothy simply in 2 Timothy 2:3, "You therefore must endure hardship as a good soldier of Jesus Christ." He gives him fair warning that tough times will come. He gives him notice that there will be moments that will test and try him but he needed to have endurance. A good soldier endures the things thrown against them up until the coast is clear and the battle is won. Soldiers not only must put on protective garments, but also have inward endurance.

Soldiers are not swayed by everything around them because they understand the importance of the mission ahead. I like how Paul would go on to tell Timothy in Chapter 2:4, "No one engaged in warfare entangles himself with the affairs of this life, that he may please him who enlisted him as a soldier." In other words, he gives Timothy the assurance that he doesn't have time for anything else that does not bring glory to God.

How is the nature of your service as a soldier? Are you bound to the task at hand or are you caught up in things that mean you no good? As a soldier, having the right weapons will help you face every battle. Ephesians 6:17 reads, "And take the helmet of salvation, and the sword of the Spirit, which is the word of God." *Today's Declaration Challenge*: I challenge you to simply fight for what you believe today. Stand up for what's right. Clothe yourself with God's word. Be strong in the faith. Declare **"I am a soldier."**
Notes

_____

_____

_____

_____

_____

_____

Day 55

"I AM AN INSTRUMENT OF PRAISE"

"Let everything that has breath praise the Lord. Praise the Lord."
-Psalm 150:6

My prayer for you today is that you would fully grasp and understand the concept of praise in your life. One might quickly gather that praise means to esteem someone or something higher than yourself. It is the act of boosting something up or speaking well of another.

From the scripture reference of today, we see the psalmist declaring the magnitude at which we as believers should praise the Lord. Psalm 150:1-2, reads "Praise the Lord! Praise God in His sanctuary; Praise Him in His mighty firmament! Praise Him for His mighty acts; Praise Him according to His excellent greatness!" Verse 6 simply reads, "Let everything that has breath, praise the Lord. Praise the Lord!"

The psalmist is clear, we should always praise God in the sanctuaries of worship. No matter where we are or how we may feel, we have a mandate to praise God. I know we live in a time where people let their level of praise be based on if they hear their favorite song or if their favorite preacher is preaching. Some people refuse to clap their hands or say amen in agreement. However, the word declares that we should always praise Him due to the breath we have in our bodies.

Would you consider yourself to be an instrument of praise? Could others look at your life and see the praises of God going forth? I'm often impressed when I see soloists, choir members and musicians, fully engaged and loving the music ministry that they're called to. Not only should we look at the musically inclined to be praise leaders but also those who don't. It should be a lifelong devotion of all of us to be instruments of praise. David declares in Psalm 30:4 "Sing praise to the Lord, you saints of His, and give thanks at the remembrance of His holy name." He went on to say in Psalm 34:1, "I will bless the Lord at all times; His praise shall continually be in my mouth."

David would give notice to us as God's saints, to always sing God's praise. Our mouths should constantly bless Him. David and Jesus were from the tribe of Judah. Judah, was the fourth of twelve sons of Jacob. His name means "praise", so praise is in the bloodline of David. He comes from a lineage of praise.

Your availability to the kingdom of God should be evident. Your excitement about God should be heard. He made you to be an instrument of His praises. Whether things are well, give Him praise. When things are trying, give Him praise. It's not a sign of lunacy but it's a sign of reverence and faith in the strength of God.

Today's Declaration Challenge: I challenge you to find a moment to praise God today. Praise Him for keeping you together when things around you are falling apart. Praise Him for replacing your ashes with beauty. Praise Him for keeping you in your right mind. Praise

Him for what did not happen. Praise Him for the things that did. Praise Him for not letting your enemies triumph over you. Thank God for creating you in all your ways for such a time as this. Praise Him for the breath you breathe. Today humbly declare **"I am an instrument of praise."**

Notes

_____

_____

_____

_____

_____

_____

_____

Day 56

"I AM BUSINESS-MINDED"

"But we urge you, brethren that you increase more and more; that you also aspire to lead a quiet life, to mind your own business, and to work with your own hands, as we commanded you, that you may walk properly toward those who are outside, and that you may lack nothing."

-1 Thessalonians 4:10-12

We can get so much accomplished when we mind the business that's ours. It sounds harsh, but it's one of the most encouraging statements that can be made.

From the time you awake to the moment you lie down at night, you are granted a few hours in the day, to take care of the things assigned to you. Whether you're a student, a parent, a career worker, a caregiver or retiree, you are allotted certain obligations and tasks to do. The only way that you're able to do them is when your focus is unwavering and strategic.

We defeat ourselves when we're distracted by something that does not belong to us. We hinder our own development when we do this. We also leave undone our own duties in the process. Paul writes to the Thessalonians about living an ordered life, he tells them, "that you also aspire to lead a quiet life, to mind your own business, and to work with your own hands, as we commanded you" (1 Thessalonians 4:11). He lets them know that peace and quiet should be your objective daily.

When we attach ourselves to things that don't belong to us, we bring conflict and unrest in our lives. Knowing what's yours and what's not will benefit you often. Even Jesus had business to attend to. He understood the importance of doing what was best for Him.

Jesus, his parents and family attended the annual Passover Feast in Jerusalem. When it was time to go home, He lingered in the city. When they discovered He was not with them, they journeyed back to get Him and found Him three days later! He was in the temple, sitting with teachers and dignitaries, asking questions and being attentive. When Mary asked Him why He had done that to them, as they looked anxiously for Him, He replied in Luke 2:49, "Why did you seek Me? Did you not know that I must be about My Father's business?"

One may ask what business did 12 yr. old Jesus have? Jesus was operating on a different level than others. He attended to God's business. He had a godly kingdom to establish. His mission was bigger than his family connections. Just like Jesus, we too must be mindful of God's business. When we take care of God's business, He then enables us to take care of our own.

Today's Declaration Challenge: What business are you focused on today? Have you done all your obligations? Many times people may ask you to help them with their trouble or issues but they forget to tell you when to stop. Knowing when to help from a distance is a key to success. Be challenged today to live a focused, quiet life. Work on the things that God has given you. If you don't do them, no one else will. If you stay in your lane, you will get where you're going faster and efficiently. You can't swerve in another lane and not cause havoc. When you operate with a godly mind, He gives you clarity to make sound business decisions. If your mind is encompassed with what God has for you, you cannot go astray. Make your declaration that today that **"I am business-minded."**

Notes

_____

_____

_____

_____

_____

_____

_____

Day 57

"I AM UNSTOPPABLE"

"For by You I can run against a troop; By my God I can leap over a wall."

-2 Samuel 22:30

My friend, let me be direct. No one can stop you! They may try to intimidate you or talk about you, but no one should ever be able to stop you from fulfilling the life that God has set out for you.

You are uniquely special. You've been blessed to do extraordinary things. You've been favored by God, way before anyone else realized it or not. You've been equipped to handle the issues of life, even when you don't understand because you know who you belong to. Knowing that is over half the battle. That's why you cannot stop, because your blessing looks good on you. Your favor only works for you.

In the scripture reference for today, we read the words of David in a moment of triumph. He has defeated Goliath, the Philistines, and escaped the hand of Saul many times in his history. He was familiar with warfare. As he had won yet again another time against the Philistines, he brings to sing in 2 Samuel 22:30, "For by You I can run against a troop; By My God I can leap over a wall." He feels unstoppable with God looking out for you, you would feel and say the same.

David had such an excitement, that he wouldn't let anything

get the best of him. Have you ever had moments like that? Moments where you felt like you could float on air. Moments like this will make even the weakest person find strength. God's power will work in your life just like this.

While you live in this day, I pray that you allow your endeavors and desires to be rooted in God. I say that because when we put ourselves in a posture to pursue greatness, peace with others and an upright life, God grants our request. Psalm 84:11b reads, "The Lord will give grace and glory; No good thing will He withhold from those who walk uprightly." Just to know that if we simply walk upright, God will give us good things. That is a blessing.

You may have just experienced the worst storm of your life or are in one right now, but my friend don't let this stop you. Your body may be well one day and ill the next but I speak life over you today to keep moving. Your friends, family and associates may be driving you cuckoo but don't stop believing God for a turnaround. Your ability to live in the middle of breakable circumstances will give you an unstoppable character. Be so unstoppable that you'll be amazed at how far you've come.

Today's Declaration Challenge: Let me encourage you to not let the problems of today to hinder you from going after everything that's in front of you. Don't allow the looks of people to stop you. Run on, even if nobody else is running with you. Leap over anything set against you. Allow your inward man to be anchored in God. With God, you can move mountains. With God, you can handle any enemy that comes against you. Find joy in what God has already allowed you to overcome. If He did it then, He'll do it again. Lift your voice and declare **"I am unstoppable."**

Notes

_____

_____

_____

_____

_____

_____

_____

Day 58

"I AM DESPERATE FOR GOD"

"As the deer pants for the water brooks, So pants my soul for You, O God. My soul thirsts for God, for the living God. When shall I come and appear before God?"

-Psalm 42:1-2

While we live, we should have a desperation for God. This desperation should be so strong that as time goes on, your entire being longs for Him. This desire can be seen all over this world, when people gather after traveling many miles to get a word, a sermon or a prophetic call to discipleship. When you have a desperation for God, you will spend time in His word, because you understand His word is His will for your life.

When you have a desire for God, it changes your attitude towards other things in life. Even the closer you get to Him, the more of yourself will have to decrease. That's why He told Moses on the mountain "Take your sandals off your feet, for the place where you stand is holy ground" (Exodus 3:5). The more of Him that you have, the less of you should be present.

I appreciate the text for today. I appreciate it because the "Sons of Korah" write this psalm out of love and a yearning for God in their lives. They had a strong love for Him. Psalm 42:1 states, "As the deer pants for the water brooks, so pants my soul for You, O God. My soul thirsts for God, for the living God. When shall I come and appear before God?" The writers liken this desperation for God to an animal, a deer that thirsts after a drink of water. If you've ever been in the middle of scorching heat in the summer, you'll understand the depths at which you hurried to find relief for your parched body.

For this reason people wake up and ready themselves for the day, pray and give God their all and thanks for keeping them alive. Psalm 63:1 reads, "O God, You are my God; Early will I seek You; My soul thirsts for You; My flesh longs for You; in a dry and thirsty land where there is no water." It's this type of desperation that you and I should look for in church or out of church. It's the pull for His presence. I pray that such a pull will always keep you close to God.

I pray that you take a moment today and ask God to show you more of His Spirit. It's in your asking that you will receive your answer. It's by way of your seeking, that you will find Him. Furthermore, don't allow people who don't want God to talk you out of your desire to have God. A closed mouth has never been fed. My prayer for you today is that you will not leave God out of your desires and desperations.

In what ways are you desperate for God? Are you able to speak of that hunger for Him in the lives of those connected to you? David declared in Psalm 23:5 "my cup runs over." He could only make that declaration as God filled him with His goodness, mercy and blessings. When you're desperate for Him, God has a way of giving more than what you asked for.

Today's Declaration Challenge: I encourage you today to regain your zeal for God. The zeal for more knowledge from Him and His presence. Don't allow anything to take away your hunger and thirst for Him. If you can be desperate for materialistic things of this world, you can be desperate for God. Your desperation for God can draw others to Him. As you need air to breathe, you need God to survive. Before you lose your cool on that job, lose yourself in prayer to a Heavenly Father that can calm that work environment. When your heart is longing for a connection that cannot be broken, open it up for God to love and let Him show you how to love others. Today lift your voice and declare **"I am desperate for God."**

Notes

_____

_____

_____

_____

_____

_____

_____

Day 59

"I AM UNBOTHERED"

"They said to Him, Teacher, this woman was caught in adultery, in the very act. Now Moses, in the law commanded us that such should be stoned. But what do You say?" This they said, testing Him, that they might have something of which to accuse Him. But Jesus stooped down and wrote on the ground with His finger, as though He did not hear."

-John 8:4-6

There will be some things in life that will try to bother you and get the best of you. Let me tell you, many times, these things will come out of the blue, unbeknownst to you and without care for your peace. It's nothing worse than facing trouble that doesn't belong to you. What matters most in situations like this, is not what is brought to you, but rather how you respond to it.

From the scripture reading for today, we see Jesus in the temple conducting and leading a lesson to those therein. As the lesson is going on, something odd happens. Scribes and Pharisees of that day, come and bring to Him a woman who was caught in adultery to Jesus to get His response. First, why they did not bring the man who was caught with her, I don't know. It takes two to tango. That's another point for another time. They quote the Mosaic Law to Jesus, awaiting His response. John 8:6 reads, "This they said, testing Him, that they might have something of which to accuse Him.

But Jesus stooped down and wrote on the ground with His finger, as though He did not hear." Jesus clearly seems unbothered by the scribes and Pharisees.

My friend, I tell you that everything that people throw at you does not call for your response. They may try to speak ill of you on your job but stay focused. They may call your phone with gossip and unwanted jargon. They may message you on social media or try to slander your name but in this life, you will need to be able to see it and not see it. It's not a sign of bowing down to the enemy but rather not demeaning yourself to the levels of others. Jesus only writes in the ground. Nobody knows what he wrote. He may have continued with His lesson or put their names there but He says not a word. The scribes pressed Him again. He gets up and simply says in John 8:7, "He who is without sin among you, let him through a stone at her first." The woman's accusers eventually drop their stones and leave.

People will try their best to bother you with the mess or issues of others, when they themselves have enough issues for a full magazine. Instead of looking at the man in the mirror, they can only view the problems of those around them rather than face their own faults. My friend, you can't be bothered by something that's not meant for you.

When you understand clearly what Romans 3:23 means as it says, "for all have sinned and fall short of the glory of God," then are you able to be on the pathway of being unbothered by the ways of this world. None of us have any room to judge another or think too highly of ourselves. It does us no good in the long run. We all have issues and faults that we're guilty of. Jesus shifted the focus of the accusers off the woman that they were bothering back to them. He deflected their judgement back to them. I dare you to do that in your conversations today when they seem to go to a place of condescension.

Today's Declaration Challenge: I challenge you to stay unbothered by what you see today. Especially if it leads to the detriment of another. Practice self-reflection today. Look at yourself in the mirror and remind yourself that God is still working on you too. When you are tempted by friends to join in topics of discussion, to slander another, think about the time that you were down. By getting caught up in the testing of your peers to bring down another, you allow the power of the flesh to win and not the Spirit. You're better than that. You've got work to do. You've got too much to accomplish to be in the middle of drama. Declare today that **"I am unbothered."**

Notes

_____

_____

_____

_____

_____

_____

_____

Day 60

"I AM THE CHURCH"

"And I also say to you that you are Peter, and on this rock I will build My church, and the gates of Hades shall not prevail against it."

-Matthew 16:18

The church is not a building. It's not a spot on the map. Yes, you may drive to a physical location, enter great sanctuaries, sit in nice chairs, sing power songs and pray until times get better but the building is not the church. My friend, as a believer in Jesus the Christ, you are the church.

I'll never forget sitting with family members and friends in their moments of sickness in hospitals, and praying with them before my departure. As honored as I was to pray, I was even more humbled, because I had to represent God and the church for them. For many people in life, you and I will be the only representation of Jesus that they will see. It's in those times you will have to confess Him as Lord over your life and share what He's done for you.

Jesus had a 'Q & A' moment with His disciples. He wanted to know what the community at-large, was saying about Him. He asked in Matthew 16:15, "But who do you say that I am?" Peter answered and said, You are the Christ, the Son of the living God." Jesus was impressed with Peter's response that He pronounces the building of His church in Matthew 16:18 "And I also say to you that you are Peter, and on this rock I will build My church, and the gates of Hades shall not prevail against it." What a great exchange! Upon Peter's confession, the church is established.

This is symbolic because based on what Peter declared, the Lord pronounced blessings over Him and the foundation of the church. What are you saying to others about God? Your next blessing could be tied to your confession. God can use your life as the catalyst for someone else's breakthrough.

There's power that is dispensed when you represent Christ. He draws others to the church, not for a show but by the witness of those who know Him and love Him therein. Acts 2:46-47 reads, "So continuing daily with one accord in the temple, and breaking bread from house to house, they ate their food with gladness and simplicity of heart, praising God and having favor with all the people. And the Lord added to the church daily those who were being saved." By exuding the nature of Christ and a genuine love and fellowship with one another, God showed His power by adding believers to the church.

My friend, be not deceived today. There will be persons that you will encounter that disagree with the church. There will be person's that don't believe and refuse to accept God and His power. They may seek to dismantle the faith you have like Herod did as He "stretched out his hand to harass some from the church" (Acts 12:1). I spoke hope to you today to not let the ways of others keep you from being the church. If everybody turns against you, and it's just you and God, you are still on the winning side. He will uphold you even in the face of persecution.

As the church, how are you shaping your connections, your communities and your areas of impact? Do you show love to those that you met? Do you offer a smile to persons that only give you frowns in return? Though I always recommend you use wisdom, discernment and conviction, I pray that your faith will remain strong enough to always exemplify the love of God.

You are who you are for divine purpose. Your living is not for selfish gain. It is to bring glory to God. It is to help others get to a blessed place. God will use you to be the light in a dark place. Do you have to be perfect? No, not at all. You do have to be available. You do have to be useful. The Lord loves you as the church. He desires for you to love yourself to be at your best. Ephesians 5:29-30 reads. "For no one ever hated his own flesh, but nourishes and cherishes it, just as the Lord does the church. For we are the members of His body, of His flesh and of His bones." He is yours and you are His. Live as the church that this world needs.

Today's Declaration Challenge: Throughout this day and every day, I pray that you walk in the authority that God has given you. I challenge you to channel your thoughts to be Christ-like. You are His agents of change. The love, grace, humility and brokenness that you show to others will change even the worst situations. The church is more than a service. It's more than a clap and a shout. It's more than a sermon. It's more than a quiet lesson. It's a lifestyle. It lives in you.

When you worship in service and gain godly wisdom and are fed the word, you better equip yourself to be the real church when the service ends. Your voice is what God needs to snatch someone out of the grasp of the enemy to new life indeed. Be the church. Open your heart to God's direction and declare today **"I am the church."**

Notes

_____

_____

_____

_____

_____

_____

_____

Acknowledgements

Merriam-Webster's collegiate dictionary (10th ed.). (1999). Springfield, MA: Merriam-Webster Incorporated.

Special Thank you to Monico Sullivan for your expertise and editorial services.

ALSO BY DERRELL DEAN

Self-Declarations: 40 Day Devotional

ABOUT THE AUTHOR

Derrell L. Dean is a licensed minister of the gospel, singer and musical director. He holds degrees from Spartanburg Methodist College and Anderson University. He resides in Upstate, South Carolina with his family.

For book presentations, additional copies or info please email thadeanslist22@gmail.com

29725216R00106

Made in the USA
San Bernardino, CA
16 March 2019